The Prayer
a true story

ADVANCE REVIEW COPY

Release: September 16, 2013

Category: Nonfiction - Religion/Inspirational

Trim Size: Trade Paperback 5.5 x 8.5

Price: $14.95 U.S. / $17.95 CAN

ISBN: 978-1-939819-00-0 (trade paper)
978-1-939819-01-7 (ebook)

First Print: 50,000

Promotion: National Publicity Campaign
500 ARC's Distributed to Media
National Trade Advertising
Five City Author Tour - New York, Chicago, Los Angeles, Dallas, Miami

Available: Amazon, BN.com, All eBook Formats
Visit www.johannpress.com for Updated Distribution Channels

Publicist: Smith Publicity
Attention: Corinne Liccketto
856-489-8654 x309
corinne@smithpublicity.com
www.smithpublicity.com

The Prayer

a true story

An Inspirational
Journey to
Miracles and
Eternal Love

JACQUELINE VON ZWEHL

Johann Press
PO Box 2428
Fort Lauderdale, FL 33303

First Johann Press trade paperback edition September 2013

The names of some individuals in this book have been changed.

For information about special discounts for bulk purchases, please contact Johann Press Sales at info@johannpress.com or visit online at www.johannpress.com.

The Johann Press Speakers Division can bring the author to your live event. For more information or to book an event, visit online at www.johannpress.com.

Book Designed by Karrie Ross

Manufactured and Printed in the United States of America

10 9 8 7 6 5 4 3 2 1

Library of Congress Control Number: 2013907028

ISBN 978-1-939819-00-0 (trade paper)
ISBN 978-1-939819-01-7 (ebook)

Dedication

This book is dedicated to all of you.

May you be blessed with answered prayers.
May your lives be showered with miracles every day.
May you find your Soul Mate.
May you experience the joy of eternal love.

May you ***know*** with *Certainty*...
This is your *Destiny*.

Contents

Preface 1

Chapter 1. The Promise 5
Chapter 2. Alone in the Park 19
Chapter 3. One Day 27
Chapter 4. Broken 31
Chapter 5. Silent Years 53
Chapter 6. A Light 57
Chapter 7. Single in New York 61
Chapter 8. First Steps 69
Chapter 9. The Dream 77
Chapter 10. A Look Back 91
Chapter 11. Israel 105
Chapter 12. Jerusalem 111
Chapter 13. The Prayer 115
Chapter 14. The Call 129
Chapter 15. Destiny 137
Chapter 16. My Miracle 147

Contents

Chapter 17. Engaged 153
Chapter 18. Coming Back 163
Chapter 19. Wedding Day 171
Chapter 20. Set Sail.... 183
Chapter 21. What is a Miracle? 189
Chapter 22. My Announcement. 193
Chapter 23. Our First Christmas 197
Chapter 24. Happy Anniversary. 201
Chapter 25. The Pinecone. 219
Chapter 26. Eternal Love 225

Acknowledgements 235
A Special Prayer 241

The Prayer

a true story

Preface

I WAS BORN WITH A PASSION FOR READING. WHEN I WAS in the sixth grade, my teacher handed out a book list with over three hundred recommended titles from which we could choose for our next book report. I made it my goal to read every single one of those books before I graduated from high school. I reached my goal just prior to starting my senior year. And then I found a new list. By the time I graduated from Penn State, I had amassed a personal library of over a thousand books.

To me, a book was the greatest treasure in the world. I could be anyone, travel anywhere, and discover different worlds in any period of history. How could anything compare to the beauty of books? I loved to hold them, curl up with them, and just simply get lost. I drank in each word, felt each character, saw new places, and traveled beyond my own reality. This was and always will be the magic of books.

Preface

My passion for reading created a need in my life to write. I began keeping journals when I was ten years old, but my serious dedication to this craft didn't develop until high school. Writing was a necessary part of my life. I did it for no other reason than I simply had to. I often wondered if my destiny was to be an author. Then, of course, I thought about some of my favorite authors. Many authors of the classics I loved had experienced tragically difficult lives. So, no, I decided I would write only for myself. I would not become an author. I was determined to get a great education and have a financially secure and stable career.

I should have learned from the many books I read that life *never* goes as planned.

Perhaps my destiny was greater than my own stubborn determination. As much as I tried to control my future, one day I found myself facing a life of terrible tragedy, similar to one of my beloved authors. I was living a life I no longer recognized, and it lay in scattered, crumbling pieces around me. During this period, I stopped reading and writing. I suppose in many ways I had stopped living. The good news is, I found a way out of this dark place, and on the other side was my new life. A life filled with miracles, my soul mate, and my greatest eternal love.

I always begin my day with deep mediation and prayers. One day during my prayers, I heard the voice of our Blessed Mother, the Virgin Mary, telling me to share my story. I never intended to be a published author, and I never meant to share the story you are about to read. Quite simply, this book was written following the orders of the One I hold dearly in my heart.

Preface

Most of the names in this story have been changed to protect privacy, except for Jacqueline and Christopher, for we are honored to share our story with you.

I am still amazed at how wonderfully surprising life continues to be. For the longest time, I could not figure out how I got here. Now, I finally understand.

This is not just my story. This is also your story. Please don't misunderstand. I know we all have very different paths, but we do share the same universal destiny. *Your destiny is to live a life filled with miracles, shared with your soul mate, and filled with the joy of eternal love each and every day.* This is the message I was told to tell.

My destiny to be an author was always there waiting for me. You will discover the same thing. Your destiny is already here waiting for you.

This is a work of pure love...from my heart to yours.

Chapter 1

The Promise

This is my favorite story in the world. I've heard it about a hundred times, perhaps more. I'm always eager to hear it again. "Momma, please tell it to me again," I'd say.

She always began the same way, "You've already heard this story a hundred times."

"I know, I know, just one more time."

She would grin and share a warm, loving smile, the kind of smile reserved only for moms and daughters. I know she loved telling me the story as much as I loved hearing it, despite her initial protests.

"When I was pregnant with you, I had a dream."

This is how it always began. I'd sit back, fall into a childlike daze, and drink in every word.

"I was surrounded by white light. There were no physical surroundings and nothing familiar. And then

I saw her: the Blessed Virgin Mary in all her awe and glory was standing beside me."

My mother paused. We both took a moment to grasp the magnitude and holiness of this revelation.

"I was wrapped in pure love. No words can ever describe such a beautiful moment."

Over the years, I've interrupted her dozens of times and asked every question a child could imagine: "What was she wearing? What did she look like? Did she look like the paintings? Which painting did the best job? How tall was she?" I always imagined the Virgin Mary would look exactly like my own mom. She would be the same exact height and have the same figure. I thought all mothers were the same. The fact is, Mom was never able to answer these detailed questions. Nonetheless, my imagination contemplated all the possibilities. I'd spend hours imagining what the Virgin Mary really looked like.

"All I can tell you is that I remember the love. I don't remember exactly what she looked like, but it was the most pure and beautiful form of love you can imagine, a love that goes right through your soul, and you can hear, see, and feel it all at the same time."

Of course, my brain could not comprehend what she meant. I never dared admit it, though. I felt I was too young to understand a concept so deep and that, magically, one day when I "grew up" I'd understand this type of love. Little did I know that children find it much easier to grasp this pure form of love than adults do. It would get harder as I grew older.

"What happened next?" I'd ask, wide-eyed, as if hearing the story for the first time.

"Our Virgin Mary approached me. She lifted her hand and held a round gold bracelet. It was the most beautiful object I'd ever seen in my life."

At this point, I'd always interrupt to announce: "This is my favorite part!" I was very impatient. Perhaps it wasn't so much impatience as the sheer appreciation of living each moment in pure joy. My mother never chastised me for all these interruptions, but she always gave me the familiar smile and continued.

"The Virgin Mary handed me the bracelet."

Now there was silence and a long pause for a moment of reflection. Her next few words would be the most miraculous gift: "This is a present for the baby. I promise to protect her all the days of her life."

My heart sang every time I heard those words.

"The following morning, you were born," Mom concluded.

I've thought about this dream often. As a child, I marveled at how beautiful and inspiring it was, but as I grew older, I wondered about the mystery. What did it mean? Why did the Virgin Mary announce my arrival the night before I was born? Was my mother happy to find out she was having another girl or disappointed and hoping for a boy? What did the gold bracelet mean? What am I supposed to do with this gift? Is she, the Virgin Mary, really protecting me "all the days of my life?" Does every pregnant woman have this dream?

I pondered these questions often and always came back to hoping it was true. Yes, hope. There's that word again, hope. It took me a very long time to learn that hope was what blocked me from manifesting the potential miracles in my life.

How could I spend my entire life hoping the Virgin Mary loved me and would really protect me all my life? Hoping that God existed, hoping my prayers were heard, or hoping everything I learned in church was real? Why was I always hoping? I had spent my entire life thinking that *hope* was the answer.

Hope was just keeping me company until I discovered the truth. Hope tried to introduce me to the secret many times, but I never listened. I clung, thinking hope itself was the answer.

We lived in Hackensack, New Jersey. Hackensack had a few Hollywood cameos. It was the target of Lex Luthor's second missile, but Superman saved us. Richard Pryor was a baseball player for the fictitious Hackensack Bulls in the movie, *Brewster's Millions.* Oh, and let's not forget, Billy Joel's song, "Movin' Out," whose lyrics wonder why anyone would want a house out in Hackensack, a town fifteen miles away from New York City. I grew up in the shadow of greatness.

Mom stayed home to take care of us kids. She was the best cook in the world. She spent hours in the kitchen, preparing the most glorious meals. We had daily treats made from scratch, soups she labored on for hours, homemade breads and jellies, grand dinners, and the most exotic desserts. I thought all kids grew up like this. Everyone's mom must be an amazing cook who prepared delicacies for their families. After all, wasn't food a direct expression of love? Every week, we all got turns having our favorite meal prepared. Dinnertime was special. We always sat down together and ate dinner as a family.

Dad was self-employed, a contractor who moonlighted as a musician. He worked hard all week and came home at exactly five p.m. every day, covered in sheetrock dust, his hands bruised, dusty debris in his hair, and all the markings of a man who's put in a hard day of labor. His treat was seeing his three girls, who ran out of the house every day when he arrived, yelling, "Baba, Baba, Baba is home." We all raced as fast as we could to grab the first hug. He would come inside where Mom had a bowl of hot water waiting for him. Dad would sit down and soak his raw, bruised hands in the water while he wove wonderful tales about his day to fill the eager ears of his three daughters as Mom prepared the family dinner table. This ritual never changed.

Oh, you might be wondering what *Baba* means. It's Arabic for *Daddy*. Yes, we spoke Arabic at home. My parents immigrated to the United States when they were in their twenties. Both were born in the town of Bethlehem. No, not Bethlehem, Pennsylvania. I can't even count how many times I've had to go through this explanation when someone asked where my parents were from. I've always had to clarify. "The real Bethlehem," I say. "You know, the one Jesus was born in." One of Dad's favorite lines was that he played kickball in the same streets that Jesus played in.

Dad lived in Bethlehem until he was fourteen, at which time he declared himself a man and old enough to earn a living. This declaration of adulthood earned him a trip to Beirut (the one in Lebanon), where he enjoyed the glorious first career of a window washer. Window washing earned him a five-flight fall from a building and a six-month rehabilitation in the hospital—all this career glory before his fifteenth birthday. His next ten years are a bit muddled for me. The only other detail I'm sure of is that he came to the United States when he was in his late twenties.

None of this information came directly from Dad. He never spoke of such things. These details came from other people, supposedly well-meaning family members who thought they were doing you some sort of favor by starting out with an ominous, "Do you have any idea what a difficult childhood your father had?"

Anyone who met my Dad would never have known he had a difficult childhood. He was one of the happiest and most easygoing people I've ever known. He always had a smile and a good joke and was surrounded by friends. You couldn't *not* be his friend. He liked everyone and everyone liked him.

Dad was an extremely talented singer and musician. He could pick up any stringed instrument and play it. He was the leader of his own band, which was booked every weekend to play at weddings and parties. For over twenty years, the hottest New Year's Eve ticket in town was the event my Dad played. He had a gift for music.

Mom lived in Bethlehem until she was about four. With the war going on, Bethlehem wasn't safe, so my grandfather moved the family to Amman, Jordan. Mom is the oldest of ten siblings. She describes growing up as lots of babies, toddlers, and kids running around and a new baby coming into the house every couple of years. As the oldest daughter, Mom had the responsibility of taking care of her siblings. She left her formal schooling in the seventh grade and began cooking, sewing, ironing, cleaning, and caring for her continually growing family at the tender age of twelve.

Mom and Dad have known each other for their entire lives. Bethlehem is tiny, and everyone knows each other. Mom's family knew Dad's family and everyone went to the same church. My family's church is in Jerusalem, a ten-minute drive from Bethlehem. If you walk down any street and announce your family's name to a local shopkeeper, everyone who hears knows who you are, your history, and perhaps some of your family's secrets and scandals. We kids used to ask my parents the age-old question all kids ask, "How did you meet?" The answer was always the same: "We've always known each other." How boring. All the other kids at school had cool stories about how their parents met. We wondered why our parents had such a boring beginning. Who ends up actually marrying someone they've known for their whole life?

Mom's version of how she and Dad ended up together is pretty simple. She came to the United States in her twenties. Dad had a crush on her and followed six months later. Initially, Mom wasn't interested, but Dad romanced, and they were eventually married. Dad's version was also simple: "Whatever your mother told you." He was very smart. He never once interjected or added his own flavor to their tale of "romance."

After five years of marriage, Tina was born. I never could understand why my parents waited five years to have a baby. Nobody did that back then. Many years later, Mom told us her secret. She did get pregnant the first year they were married. There was a terrible accident, and she miscarried at six months. Afterwards, she wasn't sure she'd ever be able to get pregnant again. Tina was her first miracle.

I came next. Two girls in a row. I'm sure this was a huge disappointment. In classic Middle Eastern culture, a woman must bear sons. When you had a boy, everyone congratulated you and you were considered somehow more blessed. If you had a girl, you'd get soft acknowledgements of sympathy, often unspoken. Growing up in a very tight-knit church community, I witnessed these differing responses on many, many occasions. Pregnant women eagerly anticipated the arrival of their children. The Sunday at church after a birth, we'd hear the big announcement from the family. If it was a boy, it was all cheers and accolades, like a ticker tape parade in New York City. The head of the family treated everyone to donuts and coffee, toasts were made, and the joy was contagious. If it was a girl, the disappointment was pervasive, like someone popping a balloon. The family received meager, forced congratulations and, of course, everyone had to offer their prayers. "Next time, may Allah grant you a son." Allah, of course, is God in Arabic.

Claudia was born next. Three girls. I can only imagine that, by then, an army of friends and family were praying that a boy would be next. The community whispered about you behind your back and speculated on what you must have done for Allah to give you so many girls. No one ever said this out loud. Of course, not; that would not be a Christian thing to do. The Christian thing to do was to keep offering more prayers. "May Allah bless this family with a son." Mom had two more devastating late-second-trimester miscarriages after Claudia. We didn't learn this until many years later.

Then one day, on Thanksgiving of my fifth year, she called the three of us girls in to have a talk. She playfully asked, "What do you want for Christmas?" I distinctly remember asking for a puppy. Yes, definitely. This is not something a kid forgets. Tina and Claudia unanimously agreed that we all wanted a puppy. As I anxiously awaited a decision on the puppy, Mom asked, "Instead of a puppy, do you want me to bring home a baby?" It was not really a question, of course.

No, I thought. Definitely no. A puppy would be more fun. What would we do with a baby? Well, it wasn't exactly a debate.

"Daddy and I are bringing a baby home for Christmas," she announced.

As soon as I realized that it was definite and she wasn't changing her mind, I gave up my dream of a puppy and started thinking about the baby.

"Where is it coming from?" was the question on our minds.

Pointing to her belly, she said, "Right here. The baby is growing inside me."

Okay, that was really gross. How did that happen? I just thought Mom was getting fat. Who knew she was growing a baby? My tiny little five-year-old mind just didn't understand. I tried, but I just couldn't understand how something like that could happen.

It was a very cold and snowy night when the neighbor came over to watch the three of us. Mom and Dad were leaving for three days. The adults told us we couldn't go with them, but when they came back, we'd have a new baby.

My brother Christian was born. Finally, a *son*. A new joy filled our house. The shame of not bearing a son was lifted. No forced congratulations or silent prayers this time: a *son* finally had been born. The cheers, festivities, and Christmas celebrations lasted well into the New Year.

We were not allowed to be like the other kids at school. They were "American." That's how Mom referred to them: the "American kids." It always confused me. I mean, all four of us were born here, so of course we were American. Not by Mom's definition. We were going to be raised according to her values, which apparently were *not* American. The American kids were allowed to do things we would never be allowed to do. We were not allowed to go to sleepovers. No birthday parties until the middle school years. No talking to boys ever, under any circumstances, not even for homework. If we needed to talk to someone in class, it could be a girl; it did not have to be a boy. We did not need any friends who were boys. Only girls.

Mom packed us "funny" lunches, otherwise known to the modern world as pita bread sandwiches.

Sending your ten-year-old child to school in 1985 with a pita bread sandwich bordered on forced humiliation. Lunchtime was a dreaded ordeal. There were the kids who got on line for hot lunch. There were the kids who had super-cool lunch boxes filled with all kinds of enviable treats. Then there was me. I had a brown paper bag. Yes, I'm not kidding you, a brown paper bag, and in it were peanut-butter-and-jelly pita triangles. I made every attempt to get to the lunchroom first and inhale those triangles before any of the other kids could see. When they saw, it was pure embarrassment. Everyone looked at me with their "gross" looks. "What is that!" Ah, the perils of being "bullied" in the eighties.

This was my family and my childhood. I was a first-generation American, but according to Mom *not quite* American, which was meant to remind me that we were being raised according to the rules from the old country. By Mom's standards, these usually clashed with the rules of the new country.

It was hard. Sometimes, it was really, really hard. I just wanted to be "normal" like all the other kids. It took a year of protests before Mom finally relented and agreed to buy American bread, also known as nutritionally-deficient plain white bread. Finally, I could eat my lunch in plain sight and stop my covert attempts to hide the shame of being different.

I wish I could say these first-generation growing pains were the hardest part of my childhood. Ah, nothing is ever quite that simple.

I have vivid memories as far back as when I was only two years old. My parents were always stunned when I recalled detailed events from such an early age. It turned into a fun game. I would describe a memory in detail from a holiday dinner, vacation, or event and then ask, "How old was I?" I'd learn I was only two or two-and-a-half at the time of that particular event.

These memories were so vivid and detailed that I always presumed they were real. Of course, they were real. How could anyone have a memory that wasn't real? There was one such memory I carried with me like a heavy burden. For years, I never shared it with anyone, but I wanted to. I wanted to tell Mom, but I needed the right opportunity.

This opportunity came shortly after my eighth birthday. I was in the kitchen with Mom. She looked somber. I was sensitive enough not to bother her, and I was surprised when she opened up to me. "Today is the five-year anniversary of my father passing away. I always get a little sad on this day."

"I'm sorry, Momma." Ah, I thought, this was the perfect opportunity. I needed to tell her.

"Momma, I have something I want to tell you." As I gathered the courage to share my burdensome secret, her look gave me permission to proceed.

"Momma, I was the last person who saw Seedo alive. He kissed me goodbye and died in my arms." (*Seedo* is Arabic for *grandfather.*)

My mother's face changed, and she looked at me very seriously. "Jackie, that's not true. You weren't anywhere near Seedo when he died. You were in the bedroom, sleeping."

"No, Mama. I was with Seedo..."

I went on to describe in acute detail my afternoon in Seedo's bedroom, our conversations, and Seedo telling me he needed to leave. He promised me he would always come back to me. His last words were, "Habibi, I love you, I love you." He always called me habibi. It's a term of endearment in Arabic. After that, he closed his eyes and gently left this world.

Mom's faced turned ashen-white as I told her my story. She was dreadfully silent and never interrupted. When I was done, she finally looked me deep in my eyes and said, "This story is not true...you were not the last person who saw Seedo alive."

By then, she looked very scared. She told me her version of what happened. "Jackie, you had just turned three. In fact, I remember we still had some of your birthday cake in the fridge. You were sleeping in one of the bedrooms. All the adults were in the living room. The moment the doctor came out and announced that he had died, you woke up in the other room and started screaming. Your screaming was so loud that it frightened all of us. You see, you were not with him."

Mom was wrong. I was with him. I'd had many conversations with my grandfather. He told me family stories, warned me in advance about people's health, announced who was expecting a new baby, and told me who was about to get married. For years, he came to me and told me everything.

That conversation with Mom was the first time I consciously realized that all my conversations with my grandfather occurred after he left this world. At first, this realization frightened me. All those memories, all those conversations—they were *real*. They were real, and no one could tell me that wasn't true. My mind couldn't quite explain it, but my heart knew they were real.

I learned one undeniable truth that day: I could talk to people after they left this world. This knowledge opened up a question which would continue to puzzle me for many, many years. If I could do that, then was death even real?

Seedo told me he loved me and would always protect me. I knew he was very real. I just didn't understand why no one else could talk to him.

Chapter 2

Alone in the Park

The screaming was awful. It had been going on for so long—hours, maybe longer. I don't know. Whenever this happened, I'd cry at first, but eventually tears do dry and my only option would be to lie quietly in bed. I'd grab my pillow and cover my ears, trying to bury my head deep enough to muffle the shouting.

This was normal in my life. At the time, I didn't know anything else; it was just how life was sometimes. I was six years old.

Early one Saturday morning got particularly bad. The pillow wasn't working to drown out the shouting, and I couldn't bear it any longer. My bedroom was close to the kitchen, where a back door led into the backyard. I knew I wasn't allowed outside by myself, but I sneaked out the back door, anyway. Their fighting was so loud that no one noticed me leaving.

I went to the front of the house and started walking towards my school park by myself.

We lived across the street from my school. I was in first grade. I loved first grade because we got to line up outside before school started, like big kids, instead of being dropped off inside the classroom like the little kids in pre-K. It was a huge milestone. Standing in line outside on the first day of school at only six years old, I felt very independent.

That morning, I went to the school playground all by myself. It was always open on Saturdays so kids could play. At the edge of the park was a large tree with a circular area of paved stone around it. I loved that tree. Every day during recess, it was my favorite spot. After lunch, the moment we went outside to play, I ran to sit underneath the tree. It was a popular spot, so getting a head start was always important.

That day, it was still very early when I got there, perhaps only seven in the morning. No one else was around. The tree—my tree, as I liked to think of it—looked different. It was sad and lonely. I'd never been in the park except when lots of other kids were there, screaming and playing. Being there all alone felt different. Then another thought occurred to me: it was quiet there. There was no screaming. This would be my new escape.

For years after that, every weekend or summer morning I woke up to the screaming, I'd sneak out the back door and go there by myself. It was my secret. I'd sit underneath my tree. Sometimes I was there for only for ten minutes, and sometimes I'd stay for hours. Actually, I had no idea how long I really stayed there on any given day. I'd just stay until I could find the courage to go back, or until I was certain the fighting would be over.

No one from the street could see me. I felt confident that I wouldn't be discovered and that no adults would come to question why I was there by myself. Not too many people were out so early in the morning, anyway.

I spent those days and hours underneath my tree fantasizing about a different life: a life in which my parents would never scream at each other; a life filled with fun and play on the weekends; a life with no Saturday morning surprises.

Even at six years old, I pondered some serious questions. I wondered why kids have the parents they have, why we're born in certain places and certain times, and why each of us has our own particular life. What if I had been born in China or France? What would my life be like? What if I had been born twenty years earlier and was now an adult? What if I had a different mom and dad? What if I never had to wake up to screaming?

After I discovered I could escape to my tree by myself, I would sit there and cry. I cried a lot by myself in those early days. The pain I felt was unbearable, and the lack of control over my life was sometimes too much. I'd often dream about being an adult. If I were an adult, I'd be able to get a job, have my own place, and never worry about anything. All I wanted was to skip my childhood completely and be an adult. I would be able to fix everything if I was older.

Eventually, I grew exhausted with wishing I was an adult, and so my fantasy life began. I'd fantasize what my life would be like according to many different scenarios. What if I was a famous child movie star like Shirley Temple? Or how about if I was a child genius ready to start college and became the youngest doctor in the world by the time I was twelve? What if I was a real-life princess and the daughter of a king? That was certainly my favorite. I spent many hours of my childhood being a princess. My imagination knew no limits; it became my best friend and my great escape from the reality and uncertainty of my life.

Life got easier. I learned to cope. I learned to block out the screaming, pretend it didn't exist, and slip into my fantasy world. My days of crying alone in the park turned into days of fantasizing about my life as a princess, and that wasn't so bad. Really, it wasn't bad.

To be fair, not all mornings were filled with screaming. Some Saturday mornings were wonderful. On those mornings, when Daddy came home, we knew he'd won. After being gone all night, he'd come home early the next morning instead of two or sometimes even three days later. On those mornings, when Daddy came home, we knew he'd won. The longer he was gone, the worse the odds were. This much I learned early on.

On the good mornings, instead of parking the car on the street and sneaking in through the front door, which no one ever used, Daddy would park at the end of the driveway at the back of the house. He'd make a loud entrance through the kitchen door and start making lots of noise, opening up all the cabinets or rooting around in the fridge. Those mornings, we knew he'd won. He'd want us all to wake up to listen to his stories and hear him boast about his winnings. Those mornings, it was safe to come out.

My sisters and I would bounce out of bed and meet him in the kitchen. We'd be rewarded with a big smile. He'd spend an hour over breakfast going over every detail of each great hand he got, how much he bet, and how he beat the dealer in Black Jack. Black Jack was the only game he ever played. His favorite places were the low-key casinos like the Tropicana: no frills, no fancy hotel, just hours of Black Jack.

The mornings he won were great. We'd each get a crisp, brand-new one-hundred-dollar bill. It was always the same. No matter how much that night's winnings had been and over the course of all the years, it was always the same: a crisp one-hundred-dollar bill.

This was another "normal" in my life. I thought every kid's father went to Atlantic City on the weekends and gave them a hundred-dollar bill if he came home a winner. Once, I asked some kids at school if they had got their hundred-dollar bills that weekend. After being shunned and receiving a stern rebuke from my teacher, I quickly learned not to ask that question, anymore. How was I supposed to know when this was the only life I knew?

I loved learning about Black Jack. It gave me a special bond with my dad. He loved talking about it, and I loved to listen. As a kid, I knew more about Black Jack than half the dealers in Atlantic City. I knew the odds for each hand. I knew strategy: when to stay, when to hit, when to double down, the best time of the day to play, where to sit at the table, and how to read the other players. I knew the lingo and hand gestures players used. I found it fascinating. This was my dad's "game." Some fathers teach their kids to play baseball; my dad taught me to play Black Jack.

As the years passed, the "wonderful" Saturday mornings became more and more rare. Having been taught the game of odds from a very young age, I knew the fifty/fifty odds of Dad coming home a winner and all of us getting our hundred-dollar bills were slipping. It was a slow and gradual decline. At first, there were a few extra mornings with the screaming and a few less "winning" mornings. The winning mornings became fewer and fewer until, by the time I was in middle school, the mornings Daddy came home a winner were so rare that I'd almost forgotten what they had been like.

Eventually, I stopped visiting my favorite tree. As I got older I replaced my fantasies and daydreaming with a passion for books. I spent countless hours reading everything I could get my hands on. I'd pick up a book and travel the world, travel through time, and get lost in a different life.

Sometimes, I missed those days alone in the park. They were my secret, the one thing I had control of in my life. My tree, my companion for years, was like a steady, reliable, and trusted friend.

Those days in the park gave birth to my ambition. I never again wanted to be so vulnerable. I would control my future. I would not become a stay-at-home mom and be solely dependent on a man. I'd never wait anxiously for my husband to come home. No, I would have my own career. I'd make my own decisions, and I would be in control.

I graduated at the top of my class in high school, then with honors from New York University.

Chapter 3

One Day

Business ethics was my favorite class in business school. A serious class, it always inspired heated debate and never failed to challenge my thinking and conventional belief systems.

I was one of the youngest students in my MBA program. After graduating from NYU, I had worked in Manhattan. My ambition was not patient, and less than a year later, I took the GMAT. I turned twenty-three the summer I began business school.

The business ethics class created a great divide between the two age groups in my MBA program. The "older" group had the traditional five to ten years of work experience and were getting their MBAs to win advanced management roles. Most of the "younger" group were fresh out of school. Academically, they were ready for the coursework but did not bring practical, real-life experience to the classroom.

Business ethics was the class in which the two groups could battle it out. It was a lot of fun. I enjoyed the open forum in which we were free to discuss ideas, debate, and be challenged by my classmates.

I will never forget one particular class. We had two guest speakers. Both speakers were alumni, exceptionally wealthy, and they had achieved wealth by following different paths. One speaker was in a traditional industry and spent decades amassing his wealth. The other speaker became an "overnight" success with a Silicon Valley internet venture that sold for a fortune. Both men had a great sense of humor, told their stories with humility, encouraged us, and took lots of questions.

It was the second speaker who captivated me: the Silicon Valley millionaire. This man was in his forties, was married, and had two young children. He spoke in detail about networking with a team of people, negotiating the venture capital money for his project, and selling it for a fortune. In effect, he became exceptionally wealthy overnight.

Up to this point, there was nothing particularly memorable in his talk. It was the spring of 1999, and overnight internet millionaires were popping up all over the place.

Toward the end, his tone and mood became quite serious.

"When I leave here today," he said, "I want you to remember something much more important than how some guy made a lot of money in Silicon Valley. This is what I want to leave you with.

"One day, you'll wake up and have everything. You'll be happy, and the world will seem great.

"One day, without warning, you'll lose it all. Your life will be shattered.

"One day, in that moment of darkness and struggle, destiny will be waiting for you.

"One day, you will have to decide.

"Will you let life break you, or will you walk through the door of destiny? Will you have the courage to get up and start all over again?"

The room was silent. The air was heavy.

The speaker continued, "Greatness is not measured by how we act when life is wonderful. It's measured by our ability to pick ourselves up from the darkest moment.

"I am not standing here in front of you today to claim that I achieved all this because my life was wonderful and easy, or that I was smarter or luckier than any other guy.

"I'm standing here because I somehow found the strength to pick myself up after the darkest days of my life. When the urge to give up almost chokes you, when you don't even want to live anymore, if you can pick yourself up and keep going, that's when you'll discover your destiny. That's why I'm here today, and that's the real secret of my success. That's what I want you to remember."

As I listened to the speaker, his words felt ominous. Later, I thought about them often. *One day…one day…* The words kept repeating in my head. I'd had a challenging childhood and survived just fine. What more could possibly happen in life?

I couldn't shake a feeling in the pit of my stomach that his words were an ominous foreshadowing.

One day, you'll lose everything.
One day, you'll lose everything.
One day, you'll lose everything.

The words kept up a beat in my mind. Why couldn't I shake this threatening feeling? It seemed to me that an angel was whispering in my ear, "Pay attention here. This will be important to your life."

I didn't want to pay attention. I didn't want loss in my life. I needed to get rid of the feeling. I used my power of positive thinking. Not me, I affirmed. That will never happen to me. My life is going to be great.

Two years later, the speaker's words came true for me.

Chapter 4

Broken

In the summer of 2001, my life shattered. In a few months, everything unraveled. Suddenly, I was in a fast downward spiral, where every day was a struggle for basic survival. Just when I would think I couldn't handle anything else, I'd face another loss.

In each instant of crisis, my first reaction was to go numb all over. It was a state of denial. The mind has an amazing coping mechanism by which it shuts down long enough that you can assess a situation and act. As I coped in the moment, I developed fears that began to paralyze me. My former confidence had dissolved, and I no longer trusted anything. I couldn't imagine any feeling in the world worse than living with fear. I was wrong. Something exists that is a lot worse than fear.

I had been so happy. I had it all: a great career working at a company I loved, a cute apartment, a steady relationship, wonderful friends. Physically, I was in the best shape of my life, and my family was nearby and doing well. Life was exactly what I wanted it to be. Everything was going according to "plan." I was on-track.

Summer is my favorite season. I always looked forward to my birthday, which is in July. I loved outdoor summer sports and swimming, and I was looking forward to this summer, in particular. I had some vacation time saved up and wanted to do something fun. At that time, my greatest worry was where to go on vacation.

The first blow came shortly before my birthday. I had been dating a nice guy for about six months. We'd met at a Penn State Alumni party during a football game. We hit it off. He was an engineer at IBM and had a good sense of humor. When his call came, I thought we'd be debating what movie to see that night. Instead, I got, "It's not you. It's me. I need some time alone and think we should take a break."

It was a shock. I wasn't in love or particularly heartbroken, but I was devastated by the breakup. I hadn't seen it coming, and I felt rejected. That's what hurt. My ego was bruised because I always thought I'd be the one to end the relationship.

I had been in love once. My first love, Chris, was the boy I dreamed about and wanted to spend my life with. My relationship with Chris had been a long journey filled with turns, twists, and a lot of backtracking that was emotionally costly.

Our relationship lasted for over six years, a high school crush that endured the long-distance college drama, sustained by summer-break reunions. Following college, we went through more drama and more time-outs, had brief reunions, and finally ended it. Each time we took a "break," I was devastated, unable to move on or open my heart to a new and healthy relationship. I was always poised to forgive and repeat the same pattern.

I had a naughty little secret: I had visited a psychic. I knew the Church disapproved, but I convinced myself one little trip couldn't hurt. I sought out someone I'd heard was gifted.

"I have one question and one question only," I told her. "Will I marry Chris?"

She said, "Yes. You will marry Chris."

I asked her if she was sure, and she repeated her original answer. At the time, I noticed a peculiar smirk across her face, as if she might be hiding a secret from me. I wondered why it almost seemed she was laughing at me. Was there something she wasn't telling me? But I didn't want to know if that was true. I had the answer I wanted. I'd marry Chris.

I had to make the relationship work. The psychic had said I'd marry Chris. So, for years, I kept hoping and wanting the relationship back. I thought it was meant to be and I could force it to work. What I got was the same movie where the lovers break up at the end.

Finally, one summer, I took a trip to the Holy Land. The trip profoundly changed me. I allowed the light of God to find a way into my soul and heal me. I found the courage to move on. I decided that only I would determine my future. I needed a new destiny. Maybe the psychic had been right: I could have chosen a life path in which I married Chris. However, after my trip, I chose a new path for my life. I put Chris in my past and began to heal my heart.

I did not want a life filled with so much emotional drama. It was the hardest decision I had ever made. My heart was beyond broken, but I ended the relationship.

I rebounded by dating a guy I met six months later, the one who was now breaking up with me. No, I certainly was not in love with him or anywhere close to those feelings. After Chris, I was not letting anyone in. I wasn't ready to get hurt again, but I did get hurt. The timing of the breakup really annoyed me. Right before my birthday? Why do guys do that? My summer was not starting as I had planned.

The second blow came a month later in early August. I was a market manager in IBM's software group. Rumors about layoffs had been circulating for months, but I had ignored them, never imagining they would affect me. I was enjoying my assignment, I liked my teammates, and I loved the industry.

It was a Tuesday morning. I had a ten a.m. call scheduled with my manager. I spent the morning preparing an update on my projects for the call.

We dialed into the conference line. My manager began, "I just sent you an e-mail. If you replicate, you should have it in your inbox." The server was slow, and my e-mail was not replicating. We waited. A couple of times I asked if I should just start with my update, but she insisted on waiting until I got the e-mail.

The server was still not replicating. We both waited on the phone in silence for about five minutes. The silence was getting awkward. Suddenly, I got an awful feeling in the pit of my stomach. Something wasn't right.

"Jackie, I'll begin, and when you get the e-mail, all the details will be in there for your review." She began her prepared speech. IBM was going through a corporate restructuring, and new strategic priorities were going into effect. Our marketing team was no longer a strategic priority. "You have been selected in this resource action."

I was selected. I was selected. The words kept repeating in my head.

I was selected?

This is how I found out I was being laid off. Very gracious of IBM to train their managers to deliver this message by making you feel special. You have been selected. Did that mean I could unselect myself? Well, thank you for this consideration, but no thank you, I don't want to be selected.

Details were rattled off and instructions given, along with a canned, required legal speech. My brain didn't hear any of it. I was in shock, numb.

My job no longer existed. It was as simple as that. I had thirty days to find a new job internally or I would be let go with two weeks' severance.

I had six figures in student loans I was paying off. I quickly calculated: even if I moved back in with my parents while looking for a new job, two weeks' severance would not pay my student loans. I was in deep trouble.

Certain moments of your life seem to move in slow motion. We've all heard that, and it's true. That's exactly how the severance call felt. One year before, I had graduated from business school with four job offers, had spent the summer traveling the globe, and I was high on life. Now, less than a year later, my career was over. Everything I had worked so hard to attain had suddenly disappeared.

After the call, I drove home in a daze. I spent two days alone in my apartment, crying. I didn't call anyone. I didn't go out. I don't even remember eating or showering. I felt like a failure. I was deeply ashamed and didn't want anyone to know. I didn't want anyone to see me.

The life I'd always imagined was gone. None of this was going according to plan.

Yes, I had a plan. I was going to have a fabulous career and be one of the youngest VPs in IBM by the time I turned thirty. I'd be married by my twenty-seventh birthday to Chris. When that relationship fell apart the summer before, I had updated my husband image to "the perfect guy." He'd be very handsome, athletic, smart, and have a wonderful sense of humor. We would have talented, brilliant, and very well behaved children. We'd live in a perfect Victorian home with a sweeping staircase, a grand master bedroom suite, a large pool, and impeccable landscaping. In the summers, we'd vacation in the Hamptons, and in the winters, we'd have a cute little cabin in Vermont where we could go skiing.

Although in my fantasy I was an executive, a wife, a mother, and vacationing all the time, I also hosted tons of charity banquets and galas in our fabulous home. I also had the body of a Victoria's Secret model. Yes, I really did believe in this fantasy; I really thought I was on a path that led to this life. It's easy to believe in dreams when you're in your mid-twenties.

The day I got laid off changed everything. I didn't just lose my job, but also, the fantasy world I'd spent my entire life creating collapsed. The fantasy world I'd created in my head was like a warm, cozy blanket. It was my best friend who got me through any bad day. I believed it. I really did.

My confidence was destroyed.

The resource action made it into the papers. Six thousand IBM'ers across different sites lost their jobs. For a few minutes, I felt a bit of comfort and not quite so alone in my perceived failure.

Then, another thought quickly hit me: I only had thirty days to find a new job internally, and I had just wasted two of them crying and wallowing in self-pity. How would I find a new job when I was competing against six thousand other people who were in the same position?

My fight mechanism quickly kicked in. I jumped into the shower, determined to get a game plan together and find a new job fast.

The third blow came. Tina called me. "You have to come home. Something is wrong with Mommy." These are the most frightening words a child can ever hear. In that moment, I experienced a new fear that, until then, had been completely foreign.

"What's wrong?"

"The doctors found a large tumor on her stomach. They think it's cancer."

I was living in Poughkeepsie, New York, a little over an hour and a half north from Hackensack, where my family still lived. After I got off the phone with Tina, I packed a bag and headed home for the weekend. I went straight to Hackensack Medical Center and found my mother hooked up to a bunch of tubes in ICU. Preliminary tests came back indicating that she did, in fact, have cancer. She would need emergency surgery to remove the tumor.

I'd never seen my mother like that before. She was sleeping when I arrived. I sat down at her bedside and held her hand. She had oxygen tubes in her nose and IV tubes in her arm. Machines were everywhere, monitoring, their lights blinking and their beepers beeping. Were the machines keeping her alive? Would she be okay without them? I began praying like I've never prayed before.

Please God, I know I've been praying a lot these last few days to find a new job. Forget all that. I don't care anymore. Please just take care of my mommy. Please protect her and take care of her. Please, I'm begging You, don't let anything happen to Momma. We can't lose her. Please, please, take care of her.

The anguish I felt was indescribable. My fear was beyond my comprehension. I had a sick feeling of losing all control. How had this happened?

Dad seemed particularly upset. At the time, I thought he was just completely out of it. He asked us kids to figure out everything with the doctors. He said he just couldn't do it.

Mom was scheduled to have surgery a few days later, once her vitals were stronger. In the meantime, we all took turns staying with her and keeping her spirits high.

I visited the hospital chapel room often during those next few days. I was so scared. I was afraid I was praying wrong. Was God mad at me for my selfishness? Had I been too self-absorbed and worried about my perfect little fantasy life falling apart? Was this my punishment? Was this one of those "life lessons" that was supposed to teach me what's really important?

I wondered how our family would get through this. None of us was coping well, and my siblings and I were fighting a lot. We were taking our pain out on each other.

The day of surgery arrived. We all stood there as she was wheeled down the long hallway. For one fleeting moment, the thought that I might not see her again ran through my mind and I literally started to choke as I held back my emotions. The next few hours were agonizing and very lonely.

God must have heard our prayers. Mom made it through the surgery. The tumor was completely removed, and she'd soon be in recovery. The doctors wanted to keep her in ICU since she had other risk factors. It was time to address the fact that the tumor was cancerous. The surgery had gone well, but she still had a long road ahead to recovery.

When I arrived, I told my family I'd been laid off. It was hard to hide it once we saw each other. It didn't really matter anymore. All that mattered was that Mom was getting better. Now that she had gotten through the surgery, I needed to drive back to Poughkeepsie. The reality was that I desperately had to find a new job. I had so much to do. By then, it had been over a week since I got the package, and I had less than three weeks remaining before I was officially unemployed.

I distinctly remember the day I came home to my apartment. I was different. A week before, my self-pity had consumed me, and its energy was still lingering in the walls. Now, I was different. I was appreciative. I was full of gratitude that my mother had made it through surgery. The appreciation gave me the strength to pursue my job search with confidence.

For the next four days, I worked non-stop. I updated my resume, met with my mentor, networked with colleagues, searched the online job database, and applied for a dozen jobs. I reminded myself of my talent, my love for the company, and the contribution I was still destined to make. I started getting interviews and then follow-up interviews.

The forth blow came a few days later. The phone rang. "Daddy had a stroke."

Just like that, my life took another nosedive. Within two hours, I was back at Hackensack Hospital.

One day, I was alone in the chapel. I went there a lot and found it comforting. It's non-denominational, of course, but I saw a small Bible in one of the pews and lots of leaflets and flyers on coping. I began to pray.

Dear Lord, please help me understand how this can be happening. Why do I have two parents in ICU at the same time, just down the hall from each other? I'm still scared for Momma and now Daddy, too. Why is this happening? Please help me understand. Please help me find the courage and the strength. If I'm praying wrong and not using the right words, please forgive me.

A priest came in. He must have seen my anguish and the struggle in my soul. I had so many doubts, fears, and unanswered questions. He said aloud, "God is listening."

"How do I know? I mean, how can I be really sure?"

"The light of God's love is infinite and always present. You don't need to speak or even think. He knows your heart."

"Both of my parents are in ICU for different things. My Mom had surgery for a cancerous tumor and my Dad just had a stroke. I'm so scared. I'm scared beyond comprehension."

The priest held my hand, and we prayed together. In that moment, I knew God was listening because He had sent one of His messengers to pray with me. I no longer felt alone.

My parents' recovery took weeks. It was a difficult time for us all, but my faith grew. Each day brought small miracles. We got positive reports from the doctors. Their vitals were getting stronger. They both recovered. They came home.

The fifth blow came two weeks later. I pulled into the IBM parking lot well after nine in the morning.

I still hadn't found a new job. I was there to pack up my office. My heart felt heavy.

I sat in the parking lot by myself for a long time. The day had an ominous feel. I turned on the radio to listen to the z100 Morning Zoo gang and get lost in a skit, one of their phone taps, a song, just anything to get my mind off my task.

"The second World Trade Center has just been hit. It is confirmed. I repeat: We've just gotten word that the second World Trade Center has just been hit. Our city is under attack! The Second World Trade Center has been hit!"

I snapped off the radio. I was angry. What a horrible skit—and in poor taste! What were those people thinking? As much as I loved the radio station, I was going to let them know that they had gone too far. They had crossed a line.

I fumed. I just wanted to relax and listen to the radio for a few minutes before going to my office for the last time, but the horrible skit had ruined it for me.

I got out of the car and headed in through a side entrance. As I swiped my badge, I noticed dozens of people standing in the hallways. All the hallways had television monitors in the corners, and people had gathered to watch something.

I looked up. There, on the screen and live, were images of smoke-filled streets, people fleeing, rubble behind them and debris flying everywhere. The headline beneath the screen read: World Trade Center Disaster. Shock. That's the only word to describe those first moments as I took in the scene. We see so many Hollywood movies with buildings blowing up, car chases, and bridges exploding, but none of it is real. We know we're just seeing a great movie, packed with lots of adventure. That's what the scene on the monitor looked like—an action thriller, one of those doomsday, end-of-the-world thrillers.

My brain was unable to connect what I was seeing to reality. I looked around me. All the faces reflected pure, raw shock. Shock. Could this really be happening? Was it some horrible prank by the news networks? I prayed:

Please, please, please, Lord. Please, I beg You to interrupt with a commercial by one of the sponsors and reveal that this is all a joke. This cannot be real.

It was real. It was the most horrible day in U.S. history since the attack on Pearl Harbor.

Only an hour before, I had been wondering how to put the pieces of *my life* back together. One blinding moment later, and *the world* had changed forever. My small life suddenly seemed insignificant. The world I lived in would never be the same. My country was under attack. No, it wasn't just my country; it was *my city*. To me, New York was the most magical city in the world. How could this be happening?

It would take weeks to learn that I had lost members of our church community, acquaintances, and a beloved former teacher. There are no words to describe such devastation.

Everyone I know has a story of that day. I've heard hundreds of them. They describe heartbreak beyond imagination. Those stories have become almost a part of our DNA; they are part of who we are.

The tragedy gave birth to many heroes, strong, brave heroes who put others' needs first and brought light to dark times. I was not one of those heroes. I was broken as I watched the events unfold.

When we encounter tragedy, two paths are always available. One is the path of victimization, of drowning in negativity and wondering *why me?* The second is the path of spiritual growth, strength, and courage.

I'm ashamed to admit that I followed the first path. The challenges of the summer, ending with this most unforeseen and horrific of tragedies, completely shattered me. Fear penetrated every area of my life. It paralyzed me. A knot formed in my stomach every time the phone rang and every time I turned on the radio or television. I was not the same woman, anymore. I was a being of fear.

A week after the September 11th attack, I was offered two jobs. I'd gone on a dozen interviews, and two of the managers had made me offers. It's amazing how quickly events can change your priorities. A month before, all I feared was financial ruin, along with the embarrassment of failure. A job was the only thing I could think about; it was all I wanted. Now, I had two job offers, but the world was broken.

Mom and Dad both came home from ICU. For Mom, the oncology tests would continue for months. Dad also had a long road to recovery. But they were home. I was relieved to be employed and to know my parents were home, but the devastation of the attacks weighed heavily on my heart. I was still consumed with fear.

I feared the ring of the phone. I feared I was a failure in my relationships and would never find love. I feared I was a failure in my career. I feared losing my parents. I feared being alone. I feared my family would fall apart. I feared for my country and our national security. I feared our nation would go to war. I feared everything. I began to fear that my fear would permanently paralyze me and I wouldn't be able to put all the pieces of my life back together. My fears controlled me and eventually they broke my faith.

For the next year, I lived under a black cloud of fear and severe depression. I lost my desire and purpose in life. I didn't want to do anything. I simply went to work, came home, ate dinner, and went to bed. I stopped going to the gym and stopped hanging out socially. I shut myself off from the world. I was miserable and cried a lot.

It was a long and dark year.

I couldn't imagine anything worse than the fear and depression that took over my life. Then, without warning, one quiet day, came the sixth blow. That was when a new adversary entered my life and he was a lot stronger than Fear. Like a new bully on the playground, he kicked Fear out the door.

I do not have a large circle of friends and acquaintances, but rather a smaller group of friends whom I love as dearly as my own family. Melissa is one of those friends and has always been like another sister to me. We could talk for hours about nothing in particular or simply watch a movie marathon on a Saturday afternoon. We had a lot in common, which is how I suppose we became friends. We shared a love of eighties movies, good books, and talking. Yes, we could talk for hours and hours and never get tired. We were both raised with similar family values and super-strict parents. We understood each other in a rare and beautiful way you only find with the best of friends.

We knew everything about each other's lives: all our secrets, family stories, relationship dramas, dreams, and hopes for the future. Well, almost everything.

There was one sacred line we never crossed, and that was talking about sex. In our very strict upbringing, we learned that 'good girls' never had sex until they were married. A girl's virtue was her greatest asset. A decade of reading Jane Austen novels deeply reinforced this belief system. In our circle even if a girl did cross that line, she never spoke about it or admitted it to anyone, not even her closest friend. It didn't matter how modern society became; in the world I lived in, this was a sacred, unspoken rule. So, Melissa and I shared everything in our hearts and talked about every subject imaginable, except sex.

One night, we were hanging out. It could have been any typical girls' night. We gossiped about celebrities and talked about boys. We both pondered our 'bad luck' in that department.

Melissa knew all about the events in my life for the past year, but I had never shared with her the depths of my depression. I knew she'd also had a difficult year. I was so self-consumed that I never guessed the depths of her depression, either. We were as close as two people could be who kept these secrets hidden in our private hearts. On this particular night, that all changed.

We were drinking mimosas, flipping through piles of tabloids, and casually watching *'The Breakfast Club'* that was playing in the background. All the headlines featured one celebrity sex scandal after another. The mood seemed light and fun when Melissa asked out loud, "Have you ever had sex?"

A knot formed in my stomach. I was not comfortable having this conversation and immediately sensed the tension in her voice. She had recently started seeing someone new, and I wasn't sure whether her question was about me or whether she just needed to talk about her own feelings. I responded with the only words that came to me: "Have you?"

She put up her right hand and the thumb of her left hand. Six fingers. What did that mean? I didn't understand. Six times? Or did she mean sixteen? That was impossible.

I suddenly blurted out, "You were sixteen!" I knew I was being judgmental, but I couldn't help it. I was stunned by her confession. I thought I knew Melissa so well. We had shared everything. How could she possibly have had sex at sixteen? It seems to me I would have guessed. It just didn't make any sense to me. I desperately hoped I was wrong.

She look at me, then, with an emptiness in her eyes that I'd never seen before. Quietly, she said, "No, I wasn't sixteen." She simply put her right hand up again and the thumb of her left hand. I still didn't understand. I felt confused.

"I was six," she whispered so softly I could barely hear her.

Tears welled up in my eyes. My lips trembled. I lost all sensation in my fingers, and I felt a violent pain pierce my heart. The room was deafeningly silent. Neither of us spoke. I was afraid to speak. I was too afraid to ask or hear any more. I was afraid that with each new revelation, the agony piercing my heart would grow larger and larger and suffocate me.

Melissa just stared at me. She was waiting for me to ask, but I just couldn't. I couldn't. Once a door like this is opened and you see what's behind it, you can never close it again. I was in denial. I desperately wanted to pretend I hadn't heard her and those words were never spoken. I desperately wished it wasn't true.

Melissa finally broke the silence, "You are the first person I've ever told."

I looked deep into her eyes and realized that although I had looked at her a thousand times, I had never *really* seen her. She was always the quiet one, introverted around others, never wore make up, never got dressed up, and never called any attention to herself. I just assumed she was naturally shy. I teased her to get dressed up. I'd ask, "Don't you want boys to notice you?" How foolish I had been. How could I not have known all those years?

I finally found my voice and asked, "What happened?"

The burden of carrying her secret alone for twenty years had finally become too heavy, and she told me everything. Melissa never told her parents. She never got any professional help.

"He was in high school, our next door neighbor, and our parents were good friends. I was six years old the first time he took me to the park. I thought we'd play on the swings, but instead he took me underneath the baseball bleachers and..."

I immediately bolted out of the room and vomited in the bathroom. I had been six years old when I began to sneak out of my house and spend my days alone in the park. Melissa and I are the same age. That same year, she was being taken to a park near her house and... I vomited again.

I don't know how long I took to pull myself together. It could have been five minutes or an hour. Time stopped. When I finally came out from the bathroom, I composed myself enough to let Melissa know she could tell me the rest.

"He told my parents he would babysit me. He told me he would kill them if I ever told them what happened. I believed him. He continued doing this to me for the next two and half years. I would just close my eyes and pretend it wasn't happening. Then one day he moved out of his parents' house, and it stopped."

I suddenly felt very cold. A shiver went through me. I was trembling. My memories started flowing back to when I was a sophomore at NYU. I lived in a sorority house and had lots of girlfriends. Early into the fall semester, right before the school load got too crazy, and everyone was still partying every night, one of my friends was raped after a fraternity party. It was a devastating and emotional incident. It frightened me so much that I spent a year seeing one of the school counselors to overcome my fear and emotionally understand how to deal with something so awful.

This was so much worse and on an entirely different scale. This didn't happen once. This didn't happen to an adult. This was a child, and it continued for two and half years. And not just a child, a *six-year-old* child. It had taken me a year of counseling to come to terms with the rape of a college friend. And this was not just any friend. Melissa was like my sister. I loved her dearly.

She was very quiet and patiently waited for me to process the information. It seems so stupid, now, but I asked the only question I could imagine: "How are you doing? How have you been coping all these years?"

She was quiet for a long time before she said, "The worst part was when I learned about HIV in school. I was convinced I had it and would die early. I couldn't get the test until I was eighteen because my parents would find out. All those years of waiting to get the test were the worst part," she recalled stoically. "The day I found out it was negative was the happiest day of my life. Before then, I was convinced I would die."

I had spent my high school years worried about how high I could get my eighties hair style bangs to stand up, and she was worried about having AIDS and dying. After Melissa shared a few more details with me, she finally told me his name.

I went through a slow and gradual process that began with denial. My denial turned to sadness. My sadness turned to pain. And my pain turned to anger. Upon hearing his name, my heart filled with anger and hatred for a man I had never met, a man I wanted to kill and make suffer a thousand times over. Of course, I wasn't capable of such an action, but I wished it. I wished it desperately.

I felt my faith in God cracking beyond repair. The other things that had happened that year had already created a few cracks in my faith, cracks that had never fully healed. After Melissa told me her secret, those cracks started to grow. Each crack became a chasm that widened every day, and it happened so slowly that I didn't realize what was going on.

This was the sixth blow, the grand-slam, knockout punch and most devastating challenge I would have to face. The sixth blow brought Anger. Anger found an opportunity to sidle into my heart and, once inside, he would not leave. He waged war against me and brought with him an army of foot soldiers named Hatred to fight on the front lines of the battlefield. I was angry at everything. He used every small detail in my life to thrust me into battle.

Anger's greatest weapon was the ability to hide. He put on a facade to hide his identity, burrowed deep inside, and wreaked his damage before I even knew he was there. For a long time, I didn't know he had waged this war against me.The foot soldiers of Hatred certainly made their presence known, but their general, the leader of this army, stayed hidden and did his damage in secret. I simply didn't realize what was happening. Yes, I had learned a terrible piece of news that deeply saddened me, but I didn't realize that these two adversaries had rolled into my life like a Trojan horse and were doing their damage furtively in the dark.

One miraculous day, years later, I was blessed with the secret weapon that would defeat these foes. Unfortunately, before that day arrived, I wasted many years of my life fighting Anger and Hatred while losing quite a few battles.

Chapter 5

Silent Years

The next four years are a blur. No one knew what I was going through, not even my family and friends. To all appearances, I was a single girl in her twenties with a great job who traveled a lot, loved the outdoors, and had a nice life. Beneath the surface, I was fighting a war. I was a functioning depressive; I appeared normal, but inside, I was utterly and completely broken.

Every time I tried to fight back, Anger and his army would re-open the door to the unspeakable event that had allowed them to enter my life. It was easy for them to defeat me whenever I remembered it. They could always get back in control.

My pain was very deep. I never thought I'd be able to defeat Anger and Hatred. Deep inside, part of me knew that my life would be over unless I could win at least a few battles. Any small victory would do, something to remind me that I had some purpose in life. Something to remind me God had not forsaken me.

I flipped through old picture albums, staring at the girl who once was me. It was no use. I didn't recognize her. Where did she go? When was she destroyed and replaced by the person who stared at me in the mirror? When did I lose all my faith? I didn't recognize anything about this new me. I didn't recognize her eyes. I'd look deep into her eyes, and they were empty. There was nothing there. I didn't know her. I didn't like her. And then, gradually, I began to hate her. I could see Anger's reflection in the mirror behind her eyes. Yes, I did hate her, and that hatred grew.

Every day for years, my routine was the same. I'd go to work, come home, and spend my nights alone, and that's when Anger and Hatred would grab me. They would join me for dinner every night and plant the seeds of destruction. Every occasional weekend, I'd go home to visit my family.

My adversaries were smart; they knew they had much less power over me when I was around others, so they patiently waited until I was alone. At that instant, a grand reunion was waiting for me.

I never prayed during those years. I didn't attend church. Anger and Hatred convinced me that church was a waste of time. Anger would whisper in my ear, "You're a fool to believe in God. What kind of God would let such terrible things happen." That's all it took for me to believe. Anger was brilliant. He stole the only tool in this world that could ever defeat him. I listened to anything he said. I blamed God. Why didn't God stop it? Why didn't God step in? If God could let something so terrible happen to a child, how was I to continue believing?

The days, weeks, and months slipped by, a blur marked by occasional holidays and the change of seasons. Icy winter was the worst, and rainy spring was a close second. Summers had always been my favorite. I looked forward to them, hoping for an ounce of comfort. The chill of autumn was lovely but ominous because of the slow decline to winter.

On many nights, I cried myself to sleep. I didn't know how this had gotten so bad. Perhaps my malady had bloomed like alcoholism: one drink, then two, and soon the person can no longer live without a few daily cocktails. The perfect cocktail for my severe depression was a little sadness, a little self-pity, a lot of anger, and a lot of hatred. I drank this cocktail every night and cried myself to sleep.

I surprised myself. I didn't think things could get worse, but one night, they did. A few weeks shortly after my thirtieth birthday, I stopped crying every night. Just like that. At first, it seemed like a good thing, maybe progress, or perhaps a strategic gain in my battle with Anger. In fact, it was just the opposite. The day I stopped crying was the day I stopped caring. It was the day I lost my energy to fight. It was the day I stopped wanting to live.

I no longer had energy for the battle. I just wanted it to be over. I did not want to live in a world I no longer had any faith in. And when I reached rock-bottom, Anger and Hatred came precariously close to winning the entire war. Somehow, at that moment, with one last ounce of energy, I fell to my knees and prayed. I had reached the brink of living hell, and finally, I started talking to God again.

Okay, if You're there and You really do love me, please help me understand. I am gorged with anger and hatred, and You know why. You know! How could You let such terrible things happen? Why didn't You stop it? Where were You? You're God. You can do anything. I just don't understand.

I don't want this life You gave me. I can't fight them anymore. I can't live with them inside me anymore. Please have mercy on me. Please, I'm begging You to have mercy. I can't do this! Don't You understand—I can't do this? Please, fight this battle for me or just grant me permission to end my suffering.

Chapter 6

A Light

No matter how much darkness you have in your life, it cannot diminish the flicker of even the tiniest light.

As I prayed for permission to end my life, a thought occurred to me. I was out of practice with my prayers. I needed a little help. I'd get my Bible, maybe find an inspiration, just something. I remembered I had a Bible in my home office. I searched for it, but the office was a complete mess and I couldn't find it. However, I found a bunch of Penn Station train schedules.

I have no idea what came over me. I looked down at the schedule and realized a train was leaving in thirty minutes. I put my prayers on hold. I needed to get out of there. I pulled a few things together and made that train into the city.

I arrived in Manhattan a few hours later. Now what? I had no plan. I started walking around. I walked towards Fifth Avenue, my favorite place in the city. I loved the shops. When I lived in the city as an undergrad at NYU, I strolled up and down Fifth Avenue countless times. Being there always made me think of Audrey Hepburn in *Breakfast at Tiffany's.* I loved the couture shops, especially, and could get lost window-shopping on one of the most beautiful streets in the country.

I strolled slowly all the way up Fifth Avenue until I saw I was standing in front of Saint Patrick's Cathedral. I hadn't planned it; it just sort of happened. In one quick, blinding moment, I had an epiphany: it was impossible for Depression to come anywhere near the radius of the cathedral! The cathedral was protecting me. I know it sounds crazy, but that's exactly what happened. I became aware that I was standing within a protective force field. Depression, Anger, and Hatred couldn't come near me. They were *not allowed* there.

I walked inside and dipped my finger in holy water. I lit a candle, knelt down, and prayed.

Lord Jesus, I prayed to your Father—or I should say our Father—a little earlier today, and somehow He sent me here. I don't know how it happened. Please help me. I can't fight them anymore. I just can't. Please, I beg you to help me. Please, come into my life and help me fight them…or bring me home.

I sat in the pew for hours. I felt safe and, to be honest, I was afraid to leave. I was protected there, and I just didn't want to risk losing that protection.

Eventually I had to leave; it was late, and dark. As I left the cathedral, I was a bit scared that the feeling of protection would disappear. It didn't. I must have carried a piece of the light with me.

I don't know what happened that day. I could never explain it adequately. My rational mind has only one explanation: the Lord instantly answered my prayer and began fighting the battle for me. I didn't fully realize it was happening.

I went home with a sense of lightness I didn't recognize, a lightness I hadn't felt in years. Peace.

I began a new routine. Every Saturday, I took the train into the city and spent hours sitting in Saint Patrick's Cathedral, praying. I sat through the masses, walked around the church, and prayed to the different saints.

Slowly and very subtly, I started to change. I was getting my life back. My work was more enjoyable, I spent more time with my friends, and I got back into a regular workout routine. They were small changes that accumulated. The Adversary and his army went into hiding. They weren't defeated yet, but by the grace of the Lord, I began my journey of healing.

After a while, something amazing happened. One evening, I realized I was laughing. I had rediscovered joy in living.

I also rediscovered the dating life.

Chapter 7

Single in New York

A guy at work had been flirting with me for months. I flirted back innocently but always maintained a safe and professional distance. Whenever he asked me out, I explained that I had a strict no-dating-at-work policy. He was cute, smart, and funny. One day, I thought, why not? I mean, hundreds of IBMers were married to each other. We were not in the same department, so I could not see any harm in it.

We went out to dinner. All night, he talked about the industry, the company, and his job. He was cute on the surface, but we had zero chemistry. I could not endure another night like that. We exchanged an amicable kiss on the check at the end of the evening, and we both knew there would not be a second date.

Every once in a while, to break up my routine, I'd take the train to New York City and work out of the Madison Avenue office. I loved the energy of the city. On one such occasion, I met a lawyer at a deli nearby. After a few "chance" encounters, we coordinated our schedules so we could meet for lunch. Not too long after that, he asked me out.

Our first date started out great: beautiful restaurant, great conversation, and we had a lot in common. Everything was perfect until the waitress was a bit late serving our dinner. My date was agitated and became demanding. After a few more minutes of cold appetizers in front of us and still no dinner, he became quite rude. I could tell he was probably an excellent litigator in the courtroom, but he was failing to get a positive verdict on our date. I politely thanked him at the end of the evening.

Who has ever been single in New York and hasn't at least once met someone on Match.com? Well, I hate to admit it, but I joined the club. The guy I met on Match owned his own small bike company in Connecticut and loved the outdoors. He lived about forty minutes from me, and we decided to meet at a national park about halfway between our homes and spend an afternoon hiking.

That date went really well. We had a great time. Hiking was a perfect setup to get to know someone, and I really thought there could be something between us. We hiked all the way to the top of the mountain and enjoyed a beautiful view. The date was going so well that I think my date just got a little too comfortable. He started unloading about his past.

He talked about his ex-girlfriend, their troublesome relationship, how much it hurt him, and what he was looking for. That was Strike One. He shared the non-negotiable list of qualities he needed in someone before he could commit his heart again. Strike Two. He went on and on. Strike Three.

I was about to give up on dating or at least put it on a time-out when I met a very handsome, very distinguished gentleman while traveling on business and seated in first class. He was the CEO of a reputable New York City bank. He was a bit older than I, larger than life, and incredibly charming.

For our first date, he arranged for a limo to pick me up from my apartment upstate. We had tickets to the New York City Ballet and had dinner at one of Manhattan's finest restaurants. It was a magical night, just perfect. At the end of the evening, he gave me an innocent goodnight kiss and asked me out again.

Our second date was on a Friday night. I happened to be working in the city that day. Since we were both downtown in the financial district, we decided to meet at the bar of a well-known hotel for a quick, pre-dinner drink. I arrived a few minutes late and found that my date had already ordered me a drink. He looked a bit inebriated.

A few minutes after I sat down, he started flirting. I didn't think too much about it until his comments turned more sexual. By then, my radar was up. Before I realized what was going on, my date blatantly asked me if I wanted to just skip dinner and get a room in the hotel. I politely told him the suggestion was offensive and that it was never going to happen. He got belligerent and started arguing with me. "Do you have any idea how much money I spent on last weekend's date? This is our second date. How long are you expecting me to wait?"

I was horrified. I did a quick reality check and decided that I had not sent any mixed signals. I concluded that this guy was just very wealthy and powerful and lived in a world where he always got what he wanted exactly when he wanted it. Just as quickly as he blew up at me, he quickly back-tracked, apologized profusely, and said he had no idea what had come over him. He turned charming again, as if it had never happened.

This behavior scared me. I'd never been scared on a date, but this scared me. I accepted the apology, excused myself to go to the ladies room, and quickly slipped out of the hotel. I never saw that guy again.

The more I dated, the more depressing the single world seemed. I'd gone out with the work-obsessed guy, the rude guy, the ex-girlfriend-obsessed guy, and the control freak, sex-obsessed guy. In a city of over eight million people, was there not one nice normal guy?

There I was, thirty years old and still single. I really wanted to meet someone wonderful, get married, have a few kids, and build a nice home together. It didn't seem that I was asking a lot, but the reality of the dating scene was proving daunting. Finally, I was putting all the my pieces of my life back together, but the one remaining battle was with loneliness.

I began the calculations. If I met the perfect guy that day, we'd have to date for one year, be engaged for one year, then be married for one year before having kid number one. It would be another two years before kid number two and two more before kid number three. After adding a year or two as a margin of error, I realized I could be forty by the time I had my third kid! That was not going to happen. My scenario also assumed that the relationship progressed along the timeline I laid out and didn't implode along the way.

Welcome to my world and my new friend on the block: Desperation. I soon learned that Desperation is one of the most popular guys in the New York dating scene. Single New Yorkers are all gorgeous, successful, smart, and witty. They *look* like they have it all. The problem is, Desperation is secretly lurking in every corner, hidden by a facade of ego, clothed in Prada, and strolling about in Manolos.

I had spent years battling Anger and Depression. By the grace of the Lord, I was finally starting to heal. Now, my dating experiences in New York were leading me dangerously close to that dark place once again. During one of my Saturdays in Saint Patrick's, I had a candid talk with the Lord about it.

Dear Lord, please help me figure this out. Why am I meeting all the wrong people? What are You trying to teach me? Let's pretend I'm very thick in the head and subtlety is not my strong suit... Okay, okay, if I'm going to be honest here, we don't have to pretend. The point is, I need a sign. Something concrete. I really want to meet someone wonderful. Am I asking too much? Just one tiny little sign. Please, give me something to help me figure out what to do.

A few days later, I received a phone call. A good friend of mine from Long Island, Todd called to invite me to a raft-up. Twenty boats were participating. A hundred of Long Island's hottest, funniest, and most successful singles would be there. I had no clue what on earth a raft-up was, but I thought that maybe it was the sign I was looking for. I cleared my calendar and the following weekend drove down to Long Island's North Shore.

I arrived at the marina very early on Saturday morning. No one was there. It certainly didn't look like there were twenty boats or a hundred people getting ready for a day on the water. It had taken me over two hours to drive down there, and I was annoyed. I finally got hold of Todd on the phone and found out that the raft-up had been cancelled. Ah, but the good news was that a friend of his was still available to take his boat out with the small group who had showed up at the marina.

That small group turned out to be twelve other women I had never met, as well as Todd and his friend, the boat owner. I probably don't have to say it but, except for Todd and his friend, this was not the demographic the rest of us had hoped for. I finally decided that a day out on the water was better than nothing.

I was wrong. A day out on the water with that group turned out to be much worse than nothing. The boat owner got very drunk, attempted to show off in front of all the women, and ran the boat aground at a dangerously fast speed. Two of the women were injured, and we were all pretty upset. If that wasn't bad enough, the boat owner didn't have insurance.

He refused to pay Sea Tow to take us back to shore and instead announced that we'd need to wait about four more hours until high tide released the boat.

I spent that afternoon trapped on a boat with twelve other women, listening to all their stories. The booze started flowing, and the stories got more and more personal. Each woman told her life story, the drama of her past broken relationships, and her current struggles. As I sat there and listened, the stories got worse and worse. The new name of the "game" was to top the previous story told. It was awful.

The tide eventually rose, and the boat made its way back to the marina very late that evening.

I had the answer I needed. It was not the sign I had been looking for, but I certainly got the message. I needed to get out of New York. My worst fear was facing me. If I stayed there, I could become like those women, bitter and miserable, complaining about all the terrible guys out there. Instinctively, I knew that this kind of negative energy would never attract the right person. Staying there would be like trying to swim upstream. The tide was too strong.

Dear New York,

I love you. You are a most amazing and magical city. You will always be in my heart, but right now we need to take a break. It's not you; it's me.

The universe has an amazing way of delivering exactly what you need exactly when you need it. A few weeks after the disastrous raft-up, I received a promotion that gave me the opportunity to live anywhere in the country. I only needed to decide where to go. Well, I loved the water. I loved summer. I loved palm trees.

I arrived at my new home in Boca Raton, Florida, on my thirty-first birthday.

Chapter 8

First Steps

Everyone I met in Boca Raton was a former New Yorker. I moved over thirteen hundred miles to learn this fact. Every new conversation started the same way: "What part of New York did you come from?" I wished I could lie and say something glamorous like, "I'm from the Upper East Side." Instead, I always told the truth. "I lived in upstate New York." Unfortunately, this turned out to be the perfect conversation killer. I had moved to Florida to get away from New York but, ironically, New York followed me.

Once I was there, I needed to create a new life. I wasn't sure where to start. How exactly do you go shopping for a new life? Moving was a big step, but once that was done, what was next? To get the process started, I went to a lovely, overpriced stationery store, where I spent way too much money on a fancy leather-bound journal to write down my goals.

I looked for the perfect setting to do my brainstorming. What could be more perfect than the beach? So, I drove to the beach, laid out a soft blanket, and enjoyed some chocolate. The chocolate was a vital component. I firmly believe one must never embark on a new life without great chocolate. I took a few deep breaths and basked in the beauty of my surroundings. Appreciation, I knew, was another key to opening up the channel of inspiration. Finally, it was time to take out my journal.

I stared at the journal for an hour and had no idea what to write. My mind was blank. Nothing. I ate some more chocolate, hoping a little more sugar would supercharge my brain.

Maybe I could open up my own chocolate boutique. How incredibly awesome that would be! Of course, I didn't have the startup capital—or the experience—and I'd probably eat all my profits. Not a good idea.

I spent another hour and a half daydreaming and getting a little sunburned. Finally, I wrote the word "Goals" across the top of a page and listed the following three steps:

Step One: Figure out My Life's Purpose
Step Two: Get in Shape
Step Three: Make New Friends

Had I really just spent fifty dollars on a journal to write that? Why was this exercise so hard? Step One was daunting. Some people spend their entire lives trying to figure that one out. What was the purpose of my life? I hadn't the faintest idea. I'd have to put that one on hold for a while. I was just not ready to go there.

Step Two was easy. I know I had just inhaled five Godiva truffles, but when I focused, I knew *could* cut down to one or two a day. I needed to join a gym, work out for at least an hour a day, and do my shopping at Whole Foods.

I didn't join a gym. Instead, I accidentally discovered one of the greatest passions of my life. My sister Tina, who lived in the area, invited me to go to a yoga class one Sunday afternoon. I'd never been to yoga and had no idea what to expect. To prepare for class, I bought a mat, a yoga towel, and some cute yoga clothes, of course.

We got to the studio early. It was just the two of us and the instructor, who was also Tina's co-worker. He was a committed yogi who practiced every day. I was blissfully ignorant of what I was getting myself into. The studio was kept at 105 degrees with 40-percent humidity. I couldn't breathe the first time I walked in. I was wearing long yoga pants and clearly wasn't prepared. "What kind of yoga is this?" I asked.

"Today we will be practicing Bikram Yoga. This practice is done in a heated studio. It's a series of twenty-six postures that we will do over the next ninety minutes." It seemed to me that ninety minutes in that heat would be impossible. While I waited for him to tell us it was just a joke, I was wishing I were at the gym, on my elliptical, with that little fan blowing in my face. "Let's get started with the first breathing exercise," he said.

Ninety minutes later, I had completed my first Bikram Yoga class. I sweated more than I thought humanly possible. My towel was soaking wet. "Ladies, you both did a great job. I'll see you both tomorrow night after work." Before I could protest, he explained, "Your second class is the most important. It's critical you complete your second class within the next twenty-four hours, because it will give your body the benefit of three or four classes."

I wasn't going back. I went home and passed out. But the following night, I did go back. I went back for a third class and then a fourth. Soon, I knew that Bikram Yoga was one of the greatest discoveries I had ever made, my key to physical well being. It became my regular practice, and it literally changed my life. It gave me mental and spiritual balance and, as an added bonus, the body I had always dreamed of having.

Step Three was to make friends. I had discovered how scary it is to move somewhere new, knowing you need to "go out there" and make friends. It's scarier than dating. Girls can be mean in their rejection. Eventually, I got the courage. I joined the Junior League.

Attending my first Junior League meeting was a frightening experience. It is intimidating to walk into a room of over a hundred women who know each other and not know any of them. Despite my nervousness, I soon struck up a conversation with another woman who was also there for the first time. Next thing I knew, the two of us met someone else.

My first year in the Junior League opened a special chapter in my life. I met an incredible group of women who became great friends, but something else happened, too. I became an active volunteer. For the first time, I regularly thought of others and considered how I could make a difference in the world. At first, I thought volunteering was about helping others. What I learned, however, was that volunteering was the greatest gift I could give to my soul. The experience opened my heart and filled it with gratitude. I learned that *sharing is the secret* to receiving the gift of gratitude. Nothing in the world brings us more joy than simple gratitude.

My first year in Boca Raton was the beginning of my healing. It was not an easy journey, and I sometimes fought it. I had doubted my ability to complete a Bikram Yoga class, but I did, and I gained one of the greatest joys of my life. When I knew I needed to make new friends, I almost let my fears paralyze me, but I stepped outside my comfort zone to discover an amazing world focused on sharing with others, which in turn gave me the gift of gratitude and joy.

I was happy. I had finally found peace in my life. But I still had to face the hardest part. I needed to go back to Step One and figure out my life purpose, and I knew I couldn't do that without a deeper connection to God.

Every Sunday, I attended a different church. I was "shopping" for a spiritual home and a sense of belonging. I was raised in the Syriac Orthodox Christian Church, but they didn't have a parish there. So, I attended Catholic Mass, Greek Orthodox liturgy, Episcopalian and Evangelical services, and a couple of non-denomi national Christian churches. I even attended a service on a beach, where everyone wore beach clothes, even bikinis, and sang the gospel to Jesus against the backdrop of the Atlantic Ocean. It was a ton of fun. Each service I attended was beautiful, but there was no epiphany, nothing like my experience in Saint Patrick's Cathedral.

I thought perhaps my expectations were unrealistic. Maybe life wasn't filled with epiphanies. What I really needed was to get back into a church and simply talk to God, which is exactly what I did.

I got into my car and started driving. I was spontaneous. I took a few back roads, exploring, and soon I found myself in the parking lot of a Catholic church. It was a Saturday afternoon. The parking lot was empty. I went inside. The church was modern and large, big enough for five to six hundred people.

I dipped my finger in the huge, center pool of holy water, bowed before Jesus on the altar, and slid into the first pew.

"Hi, God." I stopped. Oh, no. What was I doing? You can't address the Lord like that! I tried again, and this time I was more respectful.

Hello, dear Lord. Please forgive me. It's been such a long time since I've come to speak to You. I wanted to say thank You. The last time we really had a heart-to-heart chat, things weren't so good. I was in a bad place. I don't know how or why or when, but You lifted me out of that place. Frankly, I just don't under stand it. I'm just stunned by Your work. I still can't figure out how You did it. I know You're God and all, but how did You take me out of that place and make me a new person? Okay, maybe I'm not ready to know, but thank You. I know You saved my life. Because You saved my life, I know I must still have a purpose in this world. Please help me figure out what my life's purpose is and how I can serve You. Thank You, again. Oh, by the way, I'm very happy.

I'm very happy: I'd been waiting to say those words for a very long time.

As I finished my prayers and walked outside, I noticed the name of the parish: Saint Joan of Arc. Standing in front of me was a towering statue of Saint Joan, the nineteen-year-old patron saint of France who led her country through a series of victories in the One Hundred Years War. She was captured by the English and burned at the stake.

At first, I couldn't see the symbolic lesson. I stood in front of the statue, wondering what message the Lord wanted me to receive. I knew I had ended up there for a reason. What did my life have to do with Saint Joan of Arc? I wasn't leading anyone into battle. I was not a soldier. Why was I in this place, looking at this statue?

I decided I was not going to leave until I understood.

What message are You trying to send me?

It came to me. Saint Joan of Arc learned the purpose of her life through divine guidance. The Lord had acknowledged my prayer by letting me know that I, also, would receive my answer through divine guidance.

Thank you, Lord. You are the best!

I left Saint Joan of Arc with a huge smile across my face and a bounce in my step.

Chapter 9

The Dream

On my thirty-second birthday, I had an unexpected visit from my old arch nemesis, Depression. I did not invite him to my birthday—not again. How on earth had he found me? I had been doing great for the past year.

Depression had already ruined a few of my birthdays. He had followed me, harassed me, and softly whispered in my ear, tricking me into believing he's my friend. No, he was not welcome.

I spoke to him in my mind. "Leave. I don't want you here."

He responded, "What do you mean? You invited me."

"I did not invite you."

"Really? Well, your other friend did. I guess you can say I'm the friend of the friend."

Who was my other friend? Ah, I should have known: Loneliness. Boy, did I hate that guy. I thought I might be able to trick these two and run away to somewhere they wouldn't find me. So, I booked a special birthday massage at a downtown day spa. One hour of pure head-to-toe luxury should do the trick. They'd never find me there with the sweet smell of incense, glowing candles, and soft music. I was sure I'd fall into a deep and blissful state of relaxation.

But no. Loneliness followed me into the massage room and whispered in my ear, "I'm here. Do you mind if I join you?"

No, I did not want him there! I told him to go away.

He began to taunt me. "Anyone special taking you out for your birthday tonight? Oh, I forgot. That's right. Your boyfriend broke up with you a week ago, a week before your birthday. That must have stung. How many times has that happened to you? I guess you and I are destined to be best friends. I'll always be here for you, and especially for your special day. I'll invite more friends to join us. You used to love Self-pity. Should I invite him? What about Anger? Oops, I forgot. You got him under control. Okay, maybe you won't let him come back, but we're still here. You still invite us back every year."

I desperately tried to fight Depression and Loneliness. I told myself firmly that I was fine.

Depression answered: "Just keep telling yourself that, but if you're fine, why are we still here?"

For the next few weeks, I tried to dodge those two, but they kept showing up. Depression followed me all day long, and at night, Loneliness took over. I'd go to yoga and take long walks on the beach, hoping to elude them, but there they were: Depression and Loneliness. How had they angled their way back into my life? It was like a bad soap opera where none of the characters stay dead but always mysteriously pop back to life whenever the writers get bored or feel lazy.

Depression and Loneliness had some competition, though. I knew I could always find my good friend Hope in church. She reminded me that she could get rid of the bad guys if I let her. I asked her how.

"Simple. Just tell them to leave."

"That's not helping me. I've told them to leave. They won't go."

"You have to *want* them to leave," Hope explained gently.

I continued to protest. "But I do want them to leave. I hate it when they're around."

Hope continued, "I know that's what you think, but that's not how you *feel*. I know you secretly feel safe when they're around. Just tell them to leave. Tell them you don't need them."

"I don't know how. Honestly, I just don't know how. Please help me get rid of Depression and Loneliness. Please help me—just this once." I was a frustrated child trying to negotiate with the universe. Sometimes there is nothing more infuriating than getting good advice but not knowing how to implement it. "Please make this easy on me," I begged. "What should I do?"

Hope was gentle, as always. "I'm always here for you. I'm here every time you pray."

I couldn't figure it out on my own. I wanted them out of my life forever, not just for the time being. So, I took Hope's advice.

It was the night of July thirtieth, a night I will never forget. I prayed for hours. I prayed to God, Lord Jesus, and the Blessed Virgin Mary. After a peaceful night of meditation and prayer, I laid my head on my pillow. My eyes relaxed and my mind quieted as I drifted into a blissful state of deep sleep.

I "awoke" to find myself weightless and formless, sitting on a white stone bench. I had no body, but only pure essence of spirit. Even the bench seemed to be made of something besides solid matter, for it was radiating energy.

Surrounding me were what looked like clouds of pure, shimmering light. There were no objects. I felt I was part of my surroundings rather than something within them or apart from them. There was no separateness. Words cannot adequately describe this place; it was not earthly. My senses operated as one. Feeling, seeing, hearing, and smelling were all one sensation from my spirit rather than separate sensations coming from my skin, eyes, ears, or nose. Logical thought and reason did not exist, only the feeling of pure love.

Flowing over the essence of my spirit were white shimmering robes, yet I didn't feel their weight. They flowed through the air from a gentle and welcoming breeze. I was aware of a familiar scent. It was incense, like the incense I grew up smelling in church.

Most striking was the music. Melody, harmony, chant: I don't know how to describe it. It was something I *felt* rather than heard. It reverberated through my being.

Time did not exist. I don't know how long I was in that place. Five minutes, hours, days...I just don't know. Nothing I knew logically existed for me. I was at peace, a peace I had never before experienced or imagined.

As my spirit became accustomed to that place and radiated in the glow and beauty of my surroundings, I felt a pure, radiant, glowing light that penetrated every fiber of my being. Right before my spirit, the light turned into form.

The form of the light standing before me was my Lord Jesus Christ. I knew with all certainty that I was in the presence of the Lord. A river of tears spontaneously flowed from my being, and my spirit shook. Such beauty, such divinity, such grace!

Our Lord sat beside me on the bench and held my hand. No words have ever been invented to communicate the love that radiated through my spirit upon being touched by the Lord.

All I could do was cry. My tears did not stop. I could not control myself. I cried and cried. They were tears of pure, existential joy, a most radiant joy that I had never known existed. I was bathed in an essence of pure love.

The Lord was holding my hand. The miracle of the moment was beyond my ability to comprehend, even in that heavenly realm. I was humbled and awed.

I wanted the moment to last forever. I wanted never to leave. I bent down and kissed the hands that held mine. I kissed the hands of my Lord. As they touched those hands, my tears instantly evaporated into sparkles of pure, shimmering light.

Our Lord communicated to me. "I came to tell you I love you. You are loved."

I bowed my head in humility. "I love you. Please forgive me, Lord," I begged. "Please forgive me."

The Lord placed his hand over my head, and I was blessed one more time with a final message, "I love you," and I knew I was forgiven.

I woke up in a pool of tears. My pillow was soaked. I was shaking and trembling with awe. I had stood in the presence of the Lord. I was overwhelmed with sadness when I realized I was back. Oh, how I wished I could stay there forever!

I came back with a gift, a new friend. He stood beside me. Sometimes, he hugged me. I felt his presence. He promised to be there for me always. He said he would never again leave my side. My new best friend, my gift from the Lord, was Certainty. I loved him. I knew that Certainty was the answer to my prayers.

As much as I loved her, Hope vanished. It made me sad. She disappeared like a party guest who makes a quiet exit without saying goodbye to the host. I asked Certainty, "What happened to Hope? I liked her."

"I know you liked her, but you don't need Hope anymore. You have Certainty, now. You have me."

"Really? I don't need Hope anymore?"

Certainty explained, "Hope's job is done."

Clearly, I was confused. How could I not *need* hope? All my life, I had been taught that hope is everything. The churches and the Scriptures teach us about hope. Leaders preach about hope. Hope is everywhere. How is it that I don't need hope? Doesn't everyone need hope? Panic began to set in.

Certainty shared with me one of the greatest secrets in the heavenly kingdom:

"Hope has two jobs. *Hope's first job is to sustain you.* During this journey of life, Hope is the difference between salvation and ruin. Hope is the sustainer and the protector. Do you understand this?"

"Yes, Hope has saved my life from ruin. Hope has sustained me."

Certainty continued, "Great, because you must *really* understand this before I share Hope's second job, which is actually her divine mission. This is the secret many will never learn in their lifetime."

I eagerly prepared myself to receive this divine gift, this secret of the universe. "I'm ready to learn…"

"Remember, Hope's primary purpose from God is to sustain you, but her divine mission is to introduce you to me. I am the answer. Pay attention: *I am the answer to everything*."

I couldn't wrap myself around this concept, and he could clearly see my internal struggle.

Certainty was patient and explained further. "Over the years, Hope has introduced us on a few occasions.

We'd quickly meet, and you'd just as quickly forget. Or you'd blame me when something went wrong in your life, thinking I had abandoned you. Worse still, you kept letting those other guys—I won't mention their names—convince you I didn't even exist. Hope had to come back repeatedly and re-introduce us. This is her job with everyone until they unconditionally invite and accept me—Certainty—into their lives."

"Like I did when I accepted you?" I was still a bit confused.

"No, not like you. You are very stubborn! You are a perfect example of how I don't give up on anyone," he gently chided me. "Hope has been trying for years, but you kept fighting her. Only when you prayed with a poor heart did you merit the divine intervention to bring me into your life."

"What do you mean by a 'poor' heart?"

"Ah, this is one of the most misinterpreted teachings in the Bible. When the Bible or Scripture talk about being 'poor' or 'rich,' it has *nothing* to do with material possessions. This is man's foolish misinterpretation. *Poor* simply means *humble*, and *rich* is the code name for *ego*. A man can be the wealthiest person in the world, materially, and still be poor—very humble—in front of the Lord. Likewise, a man can be financially bankrupt and be referred to as rich, if he is ruled by his ego."

"What about the Bible verse, 'And again I say unto you, it is easier for a camel to go through the eye of a needle, than for a rich man to enter into the kingdom of God.' Can you explain this to me?" I asked.

Certainty laughed. "Ah, the famous verse. It is one of the most misunderstood verses in all of history. In this verse, a rich man refers to someone who is ruled by his ego. This verse has nothing to do with money, wealth, power, or material possessions."

"So, it's ego that blocks us from heaven, not money."

"That's exactly what I'm saying." With a laugh, Certainty added, "But let's be honest here. You don't exactly have to worry about having too much money to get into heaven, little Miss I-love-my-credit-cards. Which, by the way, is a different issue that we will discuss another day. It's definitely something you need to work on."

My new friend Certainty had a delightful sense of humor and knew how to keep my ego in check. Before I could dwell too long on the little reprimand regarding my foolish spending habits, Certainty refocused my attention.

"Do you understand what I'm trying to teach you? Now that you have me, you *do not need Hope*. You *cannot* have us both. You must choose. Do you want me present, or do you want Hope back? If you choose Hope, she will always sustain you, and she will always let me in to remind you I'm here, but Hope will *never* be the answer. I am the answer. Certainty is the answer, not Hope."

I sat in contemplation for hours, trying to understand the roles of Hope and Certainty in my life. I wanted both, like having two best friends to share my life journey. I wondered again, "Why can't I have you both?"

"Hope sustains you in my absence, but inside, Hope carries the seed of Doubt. That seed is the difference between us. Doubt can never remain in my presence. I can briefly visit when Hope is around, but I cannot be unconditionally present until she is gone.

"Let me repeat this so you understand: *Certainty cannot be unconditionally present until Hope is gone.*

"Hope's divine mission is to introduce us; once you truly accept me, her job is done and she will leave." Certainty could sense that I carried the seed of Doubt, and he was getting ready to leave. I was losing him. I hadn't realized what I was doing, but I was slowing pushing Certainty out the door again.

"No, no, wait! Please don't leave," I pleaded. "I just need more time to understand."

He stayed and continued to explain, "Hope is 'joyful expectation.' She is very beautiful and brings much needed light into the world. Everything you've been taught about her *is* true. I am 'absolute knowing.' This is the next level in your spiritual growth. You are no longer waiting in expectation but joyful in the moment. Living every moment in pure joy will elevate your reality to create any life you want. When you choose to have me you achieve freedom."

I was still afraid to let go. "Hope always came to me when I prayed. What will happen now?" I asked.

"I will come to you. I am the answer to your prayers. I am the source of all your miracles. I will give you everything."

"You are the secret to everything in my life?"

"Yes. I will give you everything," Certainty triumphantly declared. "There is one rule, and you must always remember it."

"I'm listening," I said, and I focused my attention.

"Ego will always try to convince you he's me. He's not. He's very tricky and doesn't play fair."

I began to wonder, "How will I know the difference? How will I know it's your voice I'm hearing, and not Ego coming to play games with me?"

"You will know it's me when your heart is thinking about Love and Sharing with others. It's *always* Ego when you're thinking only about yourself and your own selfish gain. It's *always* Ego when your actions hurt others. It's *always* Ego when you expect to gain at someone else's expense. It's *also* Ego when you only share for the recognition."

There was much to think about and understand, but I knew one thing. It was time to say goodbye to a dear friend.

Dear Hope,

I love you. Thank you so much for coming into my life when I needed you. Thank you for all the years you sustained me. I don't know how I could have made it without you. Most of all, thank you for understanding that we must now part ways. I have accepted Certainty in my life as my new best friend. Thank you for leading me on my journey and leading me to him. I know he is the answer to my destiny. Farewell.

With all my love and appreciation...

I have just learned the greatest secret in the world. This was my gift from the Lord.

"I'm pleased to meet you, Certainty. You are my new best friend. I forever choose you."

Certainty beamed with happiness. "Oh, I've been waiting a long time for you to accept me into your life unconditionally."

"Well, now that you're here, I do have one more question," I ventured as I gathered my courage. "What is the purpose of my life?"

Certainty got very serious. "For starters, eliminate *I* from your vocabulary. Your purpose in this world is to serve others."

Ouch, I had been so selfish and had wasted so many years. I felt ashamed.

"I understand you've fallen on this journey. I understand you needed time to heal and recover. Sometimes, your only job is take care of yourself, but that's never *your purpose*. Your purpose is to serve others. Don't beat yourself up. You opened the floodgates to miracles and change in your life when you started volunteering this year. It's a great start."

So, it was the volunteering? The first time in my life that I genuinely began thinking of others first. That is what created the opening to experience the miracle of being in the presence of the Lord and receiving this gift.

Certainty continued. "What I have taught you today is a miraculous gift. The purpose of your life is to teach this gift to the world. You still have a long journey ahead of you. You are not ready, yet."

"When will I be ready?"

"You will be tested. They will all convince you to abandon me, and you will fall again. You will fall hard, but I will be there with you. I will lead you to your destiny."

I was not scared. I had brought Certainty into my life, and he was the answer to everything.

With a heavy heart, I acknowledged that I had a lot more work to do. I knew this was only the beginning of a new journey. It was the beginning of my destiny.

Another thought came to me. "One more question, please."

"I'm always here for you."

"My dream…?"

"Yes, I know." Certainty said. "I can feel your heart. Heaven—what you experienced—is very real."

Such was the beginning of my new life. I stood in the presence of the Lord. I was touched by the hand of God and was given the greatest gift in the world. I was handed the secret to all answered prayers and miracles. The answer to everything.

For the next few weeks, my new best friend kept whispering to me, "It's time to go back. You need to go back. You need to go back."

Chapter 10

A Look Back

In May of 2000, I graduated from Penn State's Smeal College of Business with an MBA. I had a great job waiting for me at IBM, no financial responsibilities yet, and a wonderful signing bonus to spend. Life was good.

As soon as I got my job offer, I began planning the trip of a lifetime: a month traveling through Europe with several friends who also had jobs lined up. We booked an amazing eighteen-city tour of Europe. Following the tour, I planned to fly from London to Amman, Jordan, and spend two weeks with my family there before starting my new career.

There is something extraordinary about being twenty-five, traveling through Europe for the first time, and experiencing many different cultures in a short time. The trip would be a once-in-a-lifetime experience. Daily life and responsibilities would get complicated, and I might not have such an opportunity for quite a long time. I enjoyed every single moment of the trip and consciously tried to "memorize" each day of the journey.

The tour guide operator had a morning ritual to wake us up. Every morning as we set off on the bus to explore a new city, she blasted "Dancing Queen," by Abba. To this day, every time I hear that song, a huge smile comes across my face, and I'm taken back to the roads of my travels. Those days have a very special place in my heart.

About midway through the tour, we arrived in Rome. Although Paris unexpectedly stole my heart, I had looked forward to Rome more than any other city.

How do I describe the beauty of Rome? She's been immortalized by poets and writers as the Eternal City. If any city can be characterized as living, breathing, and radiant, it is certainly Rome. Her rich history spans thousands of years. She was the capital of the Roman Empire that ruled Europe for over seven hundred years, and many historians describe Rome as the birthplace of Western civilization. I remember her starring role in ancient history classes when I was a child. I was mesmerized by the sheer dominance of this one city. Meeting Rome was like meeting a famous movie star.

Inside the magnificent city lies another treasure: the walled enclave of the sovereign state of Vatican City and the home of the Roman Catholic Church, which was the focal point of my trip. I had chosen the only tour within my budget that included two days in Rome and Vatican City to explore these treasures.

Our day in Vatican City began very early on a bright, hot morning at the Vatican Museum. We stood in line against a massive stone wall that seemed to be endless stories high and felt a bit overwhelming. We stood in line for three hours. It was brutally hot, which I am sure made the wait seem even longer than it was. To keep our spirits up, we enjoyed getting to know visitors from other countries who shared our wait. It was a busy travel month, but I had never experienced such huge crowds.

Finally, it was our turn to enter the sacred home for art and culture within the presence of the divine. Always passionately in love with art, I was about to meet some of my best friends. Michelangelo's *Sistine Chapel*, Raphael's *Madonna of Foligno*, and Caravaggio's *Entombment of Christ* were at the top of my list. Whenever I sat in church or read the Bible, these were the images I had in my mind's eye. Now, after all these years, I was about to see them in person, and not just as images grazing the pages of an encyclopedia. (Yes, encyclopedia. That's the tool we used in ancient times to learn about things.)

Words cannot possibly describe the magic of walking through the galleries of the Vatican Museum, home of some of the world's greatest collections. The breathtaking art, sculptures, and history almost whisper in your ear, telling you the magical stories and secrets hidden there. I was transfixed. I gazed for hours at my favorite paintings, read many of the inscriptions, and had an insatiable thirst to take it all in and learn as much as possible.

Only a few days earlier, in Paris, I thought I had fallen in love while I was visiting the Louvre and the Musée d'Orsay. It was impossible then to imagine anything could rival such love, but that day in the Vatican Museum did. The galleries I walked through stole my affections. I had a new love.

After hours, we exited through a large, open courtyard corridor and arrived in Saint Peter's Square. I discovered that the space wasn't square at all; rather, it was a monumental elliptical space, wrapped by deep rows of columns. In the center, reaching straight up into the heavens, was the obelisk.

I stood there for a long time, eyes closed, taking in the moment. I was actually standing in the Vatican. Millions of people have made extraordinary sacrifices to travel to the holy city and to the very spot I stood in. I said a prayer of thanks, appreciating the moment and filling my soul with gratitude.

I could have stood there transfixed for hours, but my meditation was soon interrupted. Large groups of people were being seated, and we realized that His Holiness Pope John Paul II was about to say Mass.

What extraordinary timing and special merit! It took me a few moments to realize it was a Sunday. I had not picked up a newspaper in my weeks of travel, and I'd lost track of the day of the week. Yes, it was in fact Sunday, and I was about to hear a Papal Mass.

How could I have not realized this? How is it possible I stood on line for hours to get into the

Vatican, spent hours strolling through the museum, and yet did not realize it was a holy day? It took me an unusually long time to get my bearings and process the event. Our group followed the crowd to find seats as close as possible to His Holiness, and I prepared myself for a Papal Mass in St. Peter's Square.

There may have been tens of thousands of people in attendance. His Holiness Pope John Paul II, said Mass and addressed the crowd, speaking in Italian. I didn't understand his words, but I felt the blessing. Tears streamed down my cheeks in the joy of the moment. After Mass, His Holiness got into a car and his motorcade drove across Saint Peter's Square. He waved to everyone. I was only a few feet from the motorcade as it drove past us, and I still remember that Pope John Paul II had the most radiant smile I'd ever seen on a human being. There are no words to describe the light, beauty, and blessings of that wonderful afternoon. My heart sang.

Two weeks later, I arrived in Amman, Jordan and was greeted by the warm hugs and smiles of my family—uncles, aunts, and lots of cousins. My first cousins just from my mom's side of the family numbered thirty! I loved having such a large family. This trip was the first time I met many of them.

I had no cultural expectations for this part of my journey. My priority was to spend time with my family. I was in for quite a surprise.

Jordan is a spectacular country. Not only is it rich in history and culture but also in beauty. I visited all the tourist sites, from the glorious city of Petra to the Roman ruins and down to the Dead Sea.

I was shocked at what I experienced. After spending a month traveling through the most exciting cities in Europe and having a deeply spiritual experience in the Vatican, I was not prepared for more surprises. I was certainly not prepared to have my life change forever.

Every day during my trip, different family members picked me up and took me on a special excursion. I didn't know in advance what was planned for any given day. I didn't care; my greatest joy was knowing I'd spend the day with my family.

One afternoon, I was driven to a mountain with my aunt, uncle, and little cousins. I had no idea where we were or the significance of the landmark. All I knew was that we were going to climb a mountain. It seemed a bit unusual, but I liked hiking.

It was hot. I mean, it was really, really hot—like hot in the desert in July. Come to think of it, that's exactly where I was. The sheer agony of the heat distracted me from enjoying my surroundings until we reached the top. I wondered where we were. Why were we climbing a mountain? It was so unusual an excursion, different from all the others.

As the view slowly unfolded before me, I could feel my soul being gripped. Something squeezed my heart. What was happening? The view—I had never seen such light in my life. Where were we? What was this place? Why was my heart racing, and why was I having trouble breathing? I was quite literally having trouble breathing, and I was shaking. My arms were shaking.

I wasn't sure what came over me, but I began to cry. I couldn't help it, and I didn't want anyone to see me crying. I was afraid my family would think I was losing my mind. I didn't understand why I was reacting like that and why I was crying. It was like I found myself in a different world and the world I physically stood in was lost.

I couldn't stop crying. Silent tears. They ran down my face. Tears my mind and consciousness didn't understand. I didn't know where they came from, what had caused them, or what was happening to me. As I stood at the top of this mountain and stared at the view, the tears continued. I cried for a very long time. I had never experienced anything like it. I had never been swept by such pure, raw emotion. I also felt a hint of fear and awe: fear of not understanding what force had just come over me and awe in knowing that the place I was standing was special beyond anything I'd ever experienced.

I walked around, the tears silently flowing down my cheeks, and continued to gaze at the view. The mystery was soon revealed.

I came upon the inscription at the edge of the ridge. I was standing on the top of Mount Nebo. That's when I understood. That's when I knew why my soul was crying, my body shaking, and my lungs fighting for air. I knew why emotion had overcome all my senses and made me lose all sense of reality. For the first time in my life, I was seeing the Holy City. My soul was connected to Jerusalem.

Mount Nebo is an elevated ridge in Jordan reaching up over twenty six hundred feet. Standing upon the summit, I had a panoramic view of the Holy Land.

I had learned about Mount Nebo in Bible study classes. In the final chapter of Deuteronomy, Mount Nebo is where the prophet Moses stood when he was given a view of the Promised Land, which God had promised the Israelites following their exodus from Egypt. Moses prayed and prayed, but he never entered the Promised Land. According to tradition, the prophet Moses was buried here on Mount Nebo by God Himself.

There I was, standing on the same mountaintop and staring at the same view as the prophet Moses. I was awe-struck, breathless, speechless, and motionless. My soul had known this was the Promised Land before my mind could understand. My soul was crying. It took me a moment to make sense of my emotions, but I soon realized my tears were tears of a pure joy I had never known in my life until that moment.

This was the land Moses begged and prayed to enter. This was the land of prophets and saints. This was the Promised Land described by God. This was also the land of my family. My mother and father had both been born there, and my grandparents were buried there. This was the land of my history, my journey, and my future. That moment was the purpose of my trip.

I needed to enter Jerusalem.

Three days later, I began the journey that changed my life forever. My Aunt Marlene knew how important the journey was for me, and she promised to be my guide. The trip would need three days and would take us across the border to visit the holy sites, the village my parents both grew up in, and their childhood homes.

This trip was not on my original itinerary. When I planned my trip to Jordan, it had never entered my mind to cross the border into Israel, but something inside of me had changed. When I stood on top of Mount Nebo, I knew I would never be the same. The journey into Israel was not something I *wanted* to do, but rather, a deep spiritual *need*. My soul *needed* to make this trip even if my mind couldn't quite understand.

The journey to cross the border from Jordan into Israel is not an easy one. There were quite a few delays at the border patrol crossing, and it was intimidating for a first-time traveler into this part of the world.

I'd never had fully armed military guards check my passport so many times and ask me such a barrage of questions. What rattled me most was how young the guards were. They were younger than I was, probably none of them older than twenty.

I'll never forget the young woman who checked my passport and took me away from my family for detailed questioning. She was petite, quite beautiful, had a gentle and sweet voice, and she was dressed in full military gear, with more weapons than I'd ever seen in my life. The semiautomatic weapon slung across her shoulders looked like it had come straight out of a Rambo movie. She must have noticed me staring. I was ashamed for it, but I couldn't help it. It didn't make sense that this young, petite, beautiful girl was defending her country at a border patrol. How different our lives were! I felt deep shame for how much I took for granted in my own life.

I speak a little Arabic, but I'm not sure it helped. I tried to answer the questions in Arabic first, and then I'd stumble halfway through and switch mid-sentence to English. Honestly, I think the girl found me amusing. I caught a twitch of a smile more than once, even though she was trying to maintain a very serious demeanor during the questioning. In another place and another time, I'm sure we could have been great friends.

I must have answered all the questions well, because our passports were stamped and we crossed the border. I was officially entering the land of Israel.

After crossing the border, we found a taxi. We enjoyed a fun little game of haggling with the driver, which I had quickly learned was a required art in this part of the world. A price having been agreed, we set off to the hotel. As we drove, I tried to take in everything, but my emotions were already overwhelmed. It was certainly a different world than anyplace I had ever experienced. Everything was old, the people walking around seemed quite poor, and armed guards were everywhere. The buildings were stark, grey, and undeveloped. Street vendors were every where, selling food and other goods, and everyone was haggling.

It was different from Europe. I'd seen media coverage of the Middle East on television, but experiencing it in person made me quite emotional. I felt overwhelming embarrassment and shame. How much I had taken for granted in my life! How much I had been blessed with, yet I had too often failed to say thank you. I had not really appreciated it and simply enjoyed it. My life was so different from everything I saw around me. How different my parents' lives must have been when they were here.

How is it possible that I'd never once really thought about how they grew up? I've always known my family's history and enjoyed listening to countless stories, but I'd never really *thought* about what their daily life must have been like.

These were not the feelings I had been expecting. I had hoped for a deeply spiritual feeling, for the kind of beauty, calm, and peace I had enjoyed while listening to the Papal Mass in Saint Peter's Square. Rome was alive. The Vatican glowed with the most luminous beauty I'd ever seen. Israel was very different. My physical senses were not delighted, but my soul trembled. Something about the land shook me, something my brain could not understand.

Soon, we arrived at our hotel, which was right outside the old city of Jerusalem. We checked in and then walked a few blocks to a restaurant for a light dinner. We enjoyed a traditional Israeli meal with falafel, pickled vegetables, salads, toasted pita bread, and lots of sides. Ah, I loved the food. I also loved the warmth and hospitality of all the local people. I felt very comfortable.

I didn't sleep all night. I was like a schoolgirl the night before the first day of school. I felt too much anticipation and excitement to quiet my mind long enough to fall asleep, so I spent the entire night wide awake, just thinking.

The following morning, we entered Jerusalem. We began our day at the Garden of Gethsemane and then entered the Old City of Jerusalem through Lions' Gate. We walked the path of the Via Dolorosa and stopped to visit the Church of St. Anne and Church of the Flagellation. The path led us to the final Stations of the Cross inside the Church of the Holy Sepulchre.

Rome allowed me to experience the most radiant beauty in this world, but Jerusalem reminded me of the promise of eternal beauty in the next world.

It was a day filled with awe; pure, raw emotion; tears; blessings; thanks; and many, many prayers. I had been living my life in black and white until that moment, and it was the first time the color was turned on. I felt my eyes had been opened and I could truly see.

After a very late lunch, my aunt told me we had one more stop. We walked for ten minutes along several long, winding corridors and alleys of the Old City. She knew the streets well and knew exactly where she was leading me. When she finally announced, "We're here," I was exhausted.

We were standing in a stone courtyard. In front of us were two green, seven-foot wrought iron doors. Each door was adorned with a gilded cross, and the doors were framed within arched, stonework moldings. Another cross hung above the archway. An inscription was on the side of the door in the Aramaic writing I was growing accustomed to seeing, along with an English translation.

"Jackie, do you know where we are?" my aunt asked with great anticipation in her voice.

"Aunty, I have to be honest. I have no clue." My exhaustion was weighing me down.

"Jackie, this is your family's church. This is the church of your mother, your grandfather, and all the generations before him. This is your history. This is where you come from. This church is the home of your ancestors."

It was a lot to take in.

Just then, an elderly lady spotted my aunt and greeted her with a familiar hug. We exchanged warm introductions and greetings in Arabic. She took out keys and unlocked the church doors for us.

That was the first time I walked inside Saint Mark's Convent. I was twenty-five years old. The door swung wide open, and I *failed*. I failed to appreciate the miracle waiting for me.

We all ask the question: What is my destiny? Well, what if Destiny comes knocking and you don't open the door? Is your life ruined forever? Will you get another chance?

As I look back on the trip to Jerusalem, I see that Destiny was standing right there beside me. She led me to the top of Mount Nebo, she led me to Jerusalem, she led me to Saint Mark's, and she opened the door wide. She did all this, and I *failed* to walk through the door. I failed because I lacked appreciation. Oh, yes, I walked inside the church and prayed, but I had no idea what was waiting for me there. Destiny tried very hard, but without appreciation, she cannot manifest.

My second chance would come seven years later—seven years of unnecessary pain, heartache, struggle, and healing. If only.... If only I had accepted the gift of appreciation the first time Destiny opened her door to me. If only I hadn't wasted seven years.

Chapter 11

Israel

My plane landed at Ben Gurion International Airport on a crisp September morning. I was seated at the window and had been patiently awaiting the moment for hours. I got lost in my gaze and enjoyed the descent as the huge airliner emerged from the clouds and gently landed on the ground.

To me, flight remains a miracle. I've been on planes hundreds of times, but my anticipation of take-off and descent are always fresh and exciting. That morning, as we taxied down the runway, I felt the sun. It was a bright day. My anticipation grew. I couldn't believe I was there, or should I say I couldn't believe I was finally back. I spent hours during my flight reflecting on my trip there seven years before. This time, I would not make the same mistake.

When Certainty began whispering in my ear that I needed to go back, I knew I would be tested. I struggled to arrange the finances and vacation time. Painstakingly, I worked to combine this personal trip to Israel with some business meetings in Tel Aviv. Several times, I thought the trip would be canceled. Every time such thoughts entered my head, Fear and Doubt tested Certainty. The battles had been exhausting, but the day of travel arrived, and finally my plane had landed. My heart leapt with relief. I was there. I had made it. I was in Israel.

"Next, please." I approached the Passport Control counter and handed over my documents.

The security agent reviewed my passport for a long time. The couple in front of me had passed through easily. Why was it taking so long?

The agent asked me a long series of questions. Where are you from? What is your father's name? What is your mother's name? What is your grandfather's name? Why are you here, business or personal? Where are you staying? The agent did not seem happy with my answers. Several agents huddled together and reviewed my documents.

I quickly assessed my situation. I had arrived as a single passenger in first class. I was traveling on business for the first two days of the trip, but on personal vacation time for the next ten. I worked in sales for IBM, a high-tech global company, and I was booked on a multi-leg airline ticket that would take me from Israel to five other European cities before heading back home. Added to this, both my parents had been born in Bethlehem and had Arabic last names. Compounding the situation, I arrived in Israel on the day before Rosh Hashanah, and I was scheduled to depart right after Yom Kippur. All of these ingredients created the perfect recipe for a trip to Israeli interrogation.

"Please come with me," the Israeli guard commanded in a stern voice.

Fear. Fear. Fear. I was scared out of my mind! My stomach was doing back flips, my palms were sweating, and I had to summon every ounce of control not to visibly start shaking in front of the guards. That would be bad; it would look like I was guilty of something. I realized they must think I was a terrorist, and that wasn't good.

"Calm down. Calm down, I'm here," Certainty reminded me.

"I'm freaking out. What is going on?" I gasped inwardly.

"Just calm down. Answer all their questions honestly. Don't be cute, and don't make jokes. I know you like to do that when you're nervous, but just answer with facts," Certainty instructed me.

I started to calm down. I could do that.

"I know you're scared, but just remember I'm here," he reminded me.

I was led down a long corridor past many Israeli guards and seated in a private, stark room by myself for over a half hour. Finally, two scary looking male Israeli guards entered the interrogation room. For another half hour, they questioned me about my trip, my itinerary, my job, my religious views, my family, and my background. They asked the same questions again and again, but worded slightly differently. Then, without warning, the questions abruptly stopped, and they left.

About an hour later, a female guard entered the room and we went through the same routine. She spent a half hour grilling me and then asking the same questions in slightly different words. She, too, abruptly left the room with no explanation.

I was exhausted. I had never been through anything like it. I felt like I was in some surreal Hollywood movie, but it wasn't a movie. I was locked in a room by myself, being interrogated by the Israeli Security Agency. I thought I might lose it. My nerves were shaking. I started praying.

Please Lord, I'm afraid. These guys are seriously scaring me. I mean, I am being interrogated by Israel security. This is no joke, God. This is not funny. I know, I know, I'm sorry. I didn't mean to yell at You. Okay, please forgive me, but seriously, please step in here and help. I am really scared.

Just as I was trying to gain some composure, all three guards re-entered the room at the same time.

"We have called the hotel and all the names you have given us to verify and corroborate the information on your itinerary. We are waiting for several people to call us back. You cannot leave until we verify the information you have given us," the senior guard announced.

Then the questions began again. All three of them were interrogating me and trying to twist my words when I'd finally had enough. I lost my mind and did the stupidest thing on the planet. I had a meltdown.

"Please, stop! Do you want to know why I'm here? I'm here because I had a dream about Jesus and he told me to come here! Don't you understand that I need to be here? I don't know why. I'm not sure what this trip means or why I'm on this journey, but I need to be here. I'm not a threat to anyone. I simply came here to pray. My life has been really screwed up, and I don't know all the answers. I'm not a terrorist. I'm just a single, thirty-two-year-old woman who seriously needs to figure out her life."

What had I done? How stupid was I? I had just had a mental breakdown while being interrogated by Israeli security. They must have thought I was crazy.

The three of them stared at me for a moment and abruptly left the room. Twenty agonizing minutes later, the female guard came back in by herself. This time, she handed me a bottle of water.

"Three years ago, after praying at Rachel's Tomb, I met my husband," she confided in me. Just like that, we bonded. She *knew.* She understood. Gently, she explained. "We are still waiting for some return phone calls." She left the room again.

After five grueling hours, I was released by the Israel Security Agency. My release was contingent on very strict instructions not to deviate from my itinerary, since my whereabouts would be verified and checked every day. I was finally entering the land of Israel—under the watchful eye of the government.

The morning following my arrival, I began two full days of business meetings. I went to the corporate office park in Tel Aviv and met with the business partner team, whom I took out to dinner that night. To my surprise, I learned that the Israeli government had called every single one of my business partners while I was being interrogated, which was not exactly the kind of career attention I was seeking. After the two days of business meetings, I was on vacation. It was time to connect to the holiness of the land and figure out why my journey had brought me back there.

Chapter 12

Jerusalem

I stayed at the Dan Panorama in Tel Aviv. On Sunday morning, September sixteenth, I awoke without an itinerary for the day. After a long, leisurely bath and hotel breakfast, I made my way to the concierge. All the bus tours to Jerusalem had left for the day, and I desperately needed to go to Jerusalem. I berated myself for being foolish. Why had I assumed buses would be available all day?

As I stood there wondering what to do, I heard a man say in a thick accent, "Yes, I take you to Jerusalem. Two hundred shekels." I looked at the man who had approached me in the lobby and wondered if I would be safe traveling alone in this country. When I didn't answer, he repeated, "I take you. Two hundred shekels. It's no problem. I have car."

"Um, I don't know," was all I could mutter.

"Yes, two hundred shekels, it good price."

Dear Lord, please protect me on this journey. I desperately need to get to Jerusalem. Please send me a sign right now if I can trust this guy.

"Okay, okay, for you, I take you one hundred eighty shekels," he declared.

"Okay," I said, and I followed him out and climbed in the backseat of his car. What can I say? It was as good a sign as any.

A half hour later, my driver dropped me off at the Damascus Gate. I negotiated with him to take me back to the hotel at the end of the day.

I was finally back, standing inside the Old City of Jerusalem. I reminded myself to take a moment, to breathe, to take it in. I was standing in the holiest city in the world. "You are standing in the city of our Lord," I whispered to myself.

The first stop on my agenda was Mom's church, Saint Mark's Convent. Without a map or any idea where I was going, I started walking through the narrow, cobblestone streets. It was windy. I passed vendors and shops and open cafes. I walked through courtyards. I walked and walked until I joined a crowd moving in the same direction I was going. Soon, we came to a huge courtyard. In the back of the courtyard was an arched doorway through which people came and went. This place looked familiar. Where was I? I caught my breath as I realized where I stood. I was standing in front of the Church of the Holy Sepulchre.

I prayed there for the next two hours. Most of that time, I spent kneeling at the Stone of Unction, where our Lord Jesus' body was prepared for burial by Joseph of Arimathea. I relived the passion of the Lord, his journey down the Via Dolorosa, and his crucifixion for our sins. I imagined the agony he must have endured for our sins.

After leaving the Church of the Holy Sepulchre, I continued my quest to find Mom's church, my heart heavy and aching. I walked and walked until I finally admitted to myself that I was lost. I had no idea where I was. I had been in Jerusalem for hours. Finally, I took out my rented international cell phone and called Mom.

"Hi, Momma. Can you hear me? I'm in Jerusalem."

"Jackie, why didn't you call me when you arrived. I've been worried!"

"Oh, I'm sorry, Momma. When I arrived, I was locked up and interrogated by Israeli security for five hours. By the time they released me, I forgot to call."

Well, needless to say, this was not something any mother wants to hear when her child is traveling alone in the Middle East. It took five minutes to calm her down, but I was eventually able to ask, "Momma, please. Where is your church? Or I should say, where is our family's church? I'm lost and can't find it."

After another five minutes of yelling at me, she said, "Jackie, the church is in the Old City."

I told myself to stay calm. "Momma, I *am* in the Old City. Can you be more specific?"

"Just ask someone to help you find the Syriac church."

A group of five young men were staring at me. One approached me, having overheard my conversation. Normally, I would have been quite hesitant if a stranger approached me, but my guard wasn't up. He spoke to me in Arabic. "I can take you to the Syriac church. It's a little bit of a walk."

After we had exchanged introductions and some pleasantries, I decided to trust the young man. He led me through at least a dozen passageways and long, winding corridors. I followed him the way I had come, back through the markets, and finally we came to the familiar courtyard of Saint Mark's Convent.

"This is Ararat Street in the Armenian Quarter. This is your church." I thanked my guide and the angels who sent him to me. I never would have found the church on my own.

Chapter 13

The Prayer

My family's church was called the Monastery of Saint Mark. It had been seven years since I first saw it, but I remembered.

The monastery itself was not a distinctive building. Like most holy sites in Jerusalem's Old City, the monastery was built of stone. The only clue that it was a church was that the entrance was marked by two heavy, wrought iron doors. I remembered the doors. I remembered the gilded cross adorning the entrance and the arched stonework.

The doors were locked. No one was there. I stood there for a good five minutes, assessing my situation. It had taken me hours to find the church. It did not seem possible that I had come so far in my journey and was not able to get in.

What was I going to do? I checked my watch. It was five fifteen p.m. I had no idea what the visiting hours were. No signs were posted. I had to get in. Panic began to set in. Fortunately, I remembered my friend Certainty. I knew certainty would get me in. I prayed for his help.

Certainty, please, you've been whispering in my ear for months now that I should come back here. You've helped me in struggle after struggle to make this trip a reality. You even got me through hours of interrogation. You protected me while I traveled here with a stranger in an unmarked car, and you sent a young man to lead me here. I've gone to war with Doubt, and I have trusted you unconditionally. Let me know you're still here. A closed door? Surely, you did not lead me all the way here so I could look at a closed door. Please help me find a way to get in. I will not leave until I get in.

A couple of boys came running through the courtyard. They appeared to be ten or eleven years old. I asked them in my broken Arabic, "Do you know how I can get into the church for a visit?"

One of the boys replied, *"Stanee, stanee,"* which means, "Wait."

A few minutes later, an older woman came down a steep flight of stairs. She was dressed in black—black top, black skirt, and black head covering. She wore a huge smile, and a beautiful presence surrounded her. I wasn't immediately sure whether she was a nun, but I noticed she had keys in her hand. I silently said a prayer of thanks. My good friend Certainty had come through for me once again.

She said hello in Arabic. *"Mar ha ba."*

"Mar ha ba," I replied. I introduced myself. When she heard my family name, she lit up.

"Yes, of course. I know of your family, both your mother's and father's sides. Would you like to visit the church?"

Trying to restrain my emotions, I said as calmly as I could, "Yes. Yes, please. I've traveled a long way to come here, and I would love to have a few minutes inside to pray."

This lovely lady, an angel summoned by my prayer, opened the doors and led me inside. A blanket of love washed over me as I walked through the doors taking in my surroundings.

Inside the entrance was an inscription: *"This is the house of Mary, mother of John also called Mark. The apostles consecrated it as a church after the name of Mary the God-bearer. It was consecrated as a Church in 73 A.D. after King Titus destroyed Jerusalem."*

Another plaque bore an inscription in Aramaic. I recognized the letters from liturgy books in church, but I certainly couldn't read Aramaic.

"Would you like to hear a history of the church?" the lady asked me.

"Yes, please."

"This is the house of Mary and the Upper Room is where our Lord held his Last Supper. Many miracles and holy events have taken place here. It was here that our Lord Jesus Christ washed the feet of his disciples."

She paused. I took in each word, attempting to fathom the holiness of the ground I stood on and of the walls surrounding me. This time, I remembered to fill my soul with appreciation and give thanks.

Thank you dear Lord. Thank You, thank You, thank You. Thank You for bringing me here. Thank You a million times over.

What stories could these walls tell me if they could talk? What secrets do they hold? I ran my hand over the stone wall. Did our Lord's hand touch this same wall? I tried to imagine it.

The church was very small, with only a handful of pews on each side. I couldn't imagine more than thirty or forty people being able to fit in there at once.

I sat down in one of the pews and was jolted by a different path of thought. This was the church of my mother and father, and my grandfather, and his grandparents before him. It was where I came from. It was who I am. I'm not just visiting a holy site in Jerusalem; this is *who I am*. These walls tell the history of my own family and where I come from. I suppose it's a miracle in itself that we have survived all these hundreds of years.

Jerusalem today is divided among the Israeli Jews, the Palestinian Muslims, and the Christians, the latter of whom are a tiny minority, perhaps only three or four percent of the population. Whenever kids in school had asked me where I was from, I found it a difficult question to answer. It was complicated to explain the division of land by religion, politics, history, and belief systems. Perhaps, until that moment, I had never really understood the answer myself, so how could I have explained it?

My self-reflection was interrupted when the lovely lady continued her history of the church. "This is the site where Jesus appeared to the disciples after the Resurrection and where his mother and the disciples waited in prayer between Ascension and Pentecost. Also, according to our tradition, this is where the priesthood was instituted and the first church of Christianity was established and dedicated to the name of our Mother of God. This is why sections of our liturgy to this day are still in Aramaic. Aramaic is the language that was spoken by our Lord."

My thoughts drifted a little. I needed to refresh my Bible studies and learn more about the period between Ascension and Pentecost. At that moment, I finally understood something that had perplexed me all my life. When I was a child, I always got antsy and bored listening to a three-hour liturgy every Sunday in a different language. I wondered why the priests didn't just say the prayers in English so that we would understand. Now, I realized that they kept the Aramaic language alive so that they could say the prayers in the language our Lord spoke.

"This is also where the Holy Virgin Mary lived after the crucifixion and where she was baptized. Over here is her baptismal basin."

The lady led me to the site where the greatest miracles of my life would be manifested. I was standing in front of the holy icon of the Virgin Mary. She was tucked away, hidden, and protected by an ornate gold canopy. Within the canopy, hidden under a cover, was the baptismal basin. I stood there, mesmerized by the icon of the Virgin.

She continued, "The icon of the Virgin Mary was painted by Saint Luke the Evangelist. He painted it from life, that is, while the Blessed Mary was still alive. This is the oldest painting in the world of her actual image."

I'd seen hundreds of paintings of the Blessed Mother, but never anything like this. It wasn't a painting; she was *alive*. She was there. I could *feel* her presence. I could see inside her eyes, and she was there with me. Again, I felt a blanket of pure love. It took me a few more moments before I could even begin to comprehend how special and holy this moment was in my life.

The lady from the church could see the questions in my eyes, and I believe she could sense my awe. After she had given me a few moments to take in what I was seeing, she asked, "Would you like to hear a few stories?"

"Of course." I sat down on a pew in front of the icon and eagerly prepared to listen.

"Many, many, miracles throughout our history are associated with the icon of the Virgin. She has always protected this site and granted many graces and blessings to those who have visited her.

"One of the first miracles is simply that this is her *home*. Throughout the hundreds of years of our history, there have been a number of attempts to steal her and take her to another country. Always, within less than a day, she miraculously appeared back home in this spot.

"And here is the second miracle." She left a long pause to make sure I was listening intently.

"Come here," she whispered gently. She led me to a small altar of candles next to the icon.

"Light a candle."

I did as instructed and lit a candle.

"Now, pray to her. She will grant you any miracle you pray for with a pure heart. This I promise you."

I was fighting back tears, completely overwhelmed with emotion. "Pray to her. She will grant you any miracle you pray for with a pure heart." The words penetrated my soul. I kept repeating them.

The lady left the church to give me some time alone to pray.

There I was, completely alone in one of the holiest sites in the world. *Pray. She will grant you a miracle.* These words kept going through my mind.

I wasn't ready. I didn't know how to pray. I didn't know what to do. I knew what my heart wanted, what I wanted more than anything I could imagine, what I ached for, but I couldn't bring myself to pray for me. There was a battle in my heart. Wasn't that why I had come here, to pray for a miracle? No, that wasn't me anymore. I was different. I couldn't explain it, but I just wasn't the same person who woke up that morning in my hotel room.

I started thinking about my family, my close friends, and even this tiny little piece of the world that thousands if not millions of people have fought over since the beginning of time. Could I really stand there and pray just for myself when so much was happening around me?

I got one prayer...one miracle. That was the promise.

I desperately wanted a miracle in my own life. I knew what I wanted. I knew why I had come there but—Certainty showed up. He whispered in my ear.

"Remember what I taught you: It's me only if you think of sharing with others first; and it's that other guy, Ego, when you're only thinking of yourself. Trust me. Believe me. You only need me. Remember, you must always think of others first. That's the only way you know it's me."

That was the reminder I needed. I was ready.

Dear Holy Mother, Blessed Virgin Mary, Mother of our Lord,

I humbly beg you to grant me this miracle. I beg of you to bless your children—all of your children who live within these city walls of blessed Jerusalem—with love and peace in their hearts for each other. May the Jews, Christians, and Muslim brothers and sisters love each other unconditionally as the Lord loves all of us. This is the miracle I beg of you.

That was my prayer. I continued to stand in front of the icon of the Virgin, and I was soon crying uncontrollably. I cried and cried. There was so much more in my heart. There was so much more I had to pray for.

My prayer is for Jerusalem, for peace in this world, but I humbly beg you to also let me pray for those I love. Please grant peace, love, prosperity, health, and blessings to….

I named all the members of my family, my friends, and my community. I prayed for the world and my family with every ounce of my soul and heart.

After a while, a moment of confusion crept in, and I didn't know what to do.

"Please, please, Certainty, come back to me. What should I do?"

"I'm here," he replied. "I understand and know what you're struggling with. You want to say a prayer for yourself. It's okay. You can. You genuinely put others first, and now you can say your own prayer."

"Are you sure? How do I know this isn't Ego trying to trick me?"

"Ask your heart if you genuinely wish that your prayer for others be answered first, before your own, even if yours is never answered. If your heart can genuinely wish that, then you know it's me. That's who I am. My job is to constantly remind you to think of others first. My presence is guaranteed in your life when you are sending love and sharing with others."

I thought about these words for a long time. Being completely honest, did I genuinely wish for peace in this world and blessings for all those I loved even if it meant my prayer would never be answered?

I broke down and wept in an agony I had never known in my life. I stood there alone. I wept and wept. My head fell against the basin in which our blessed Mother was baptized, and I just wept. My tears seemed to know no limits.

Every fear, doubt, pain, and hurt I had ever felt in my life came to the surface. All the broken moments and shattered dreams came rushing back to me, and I wept for them all.

Then, without warning, the greatest battle I had ever faced in my life came to the surface: Anger and his army of Hatred. Along with these two whom I had spent so many years of my life fighting, the man who brought them into my life came back into my consciousness. The person who stole innocence and shattered for me all beauty, hope, and joy in the world. For years, all I wanted was for that man to suffer a thousand times over, suffer more agony than any other person in this world. I wanted him to know only pain and, finally, to cease living.

I stared into the eyes of my Virgin Mother, and she washed me of all the pain. She took it all away. Gone. Years of battling and hating, and she took it all away. She fought the battle for me and saved my life. She gave me the gift I never asked for because I did not know I wanted it. The gift was Forgiveness. The Virgin spoke to me the words of her Son, "Forgive them, they know not what they do." In that moment, I was healed and I forgave. I completely forgave the worst pain I ever learned about. I did more than just forgive. I prayed for the soul of the man who had brought this pain.

And so it was that Forgiveness defeated the greatest adversary who ever waged war against me. Forgiveness completely obliterated Anger and his army of Hatred. Forgiveness saved my life. The war was finally over, and I had won.

Please forgive me my anger and hatred. Please forgive me for all those years I wasted. I pray for this man's soul. I genuinely pray for his soul.

And I pray for my dear friend, who suffered this unspeakable event in her life. Please, I beg you to bless her with a healed life of pure unconditional love and joy.

I am so sorry I failed to learn the lessons you have repeatedly tried to teach me. I am so sorry it's taken me this long. I BEG you, please forgive me.

I wept like a small child who was standing in front of her mother for the first time. I wept and wept. I don't know where it all came from. I don't know what came over me. I don't know what happened on that day, in that moment. I was touched by the hand of the Holy Spirit, and my weeping cleansed me of all the pain I had ever carried. She wiped away all my tears.

I continued to stand in front of the icon of the Virgin Mary. In her eyes, I could see pure, unconditional love. She loved me, and all she wanted was for me to love others as much as she loved me. Yes, I had Certainty in my heart. I wanted my prayers for peace in Jerusalem and blessings for my family and friends to be answered *first*. Yes—and this was the most difficult moment of my life—I did want the soul of the person who committed the unspeakable to be saved. The most agonizing moment I ever faced. *Yes, please save his lost soul.* Even if it meant that my personal prayer would never be answered, the other prayers came *first*.

My Blessed Mother...

I couldn't do it. Why couldn't I do it? Why was I so afraid to pray for myself. Certainty whispered in my heart, "I'm here, and I love you. Go ahead. Say your prayer."

My dear Blessed Mother, I pray for Jerusalem, for my family and friends, and for the redemption of that man's soul. Please forgive me all my sins. Please, I beg you to forgive me. Thank you for healing my heart and loving me.

I could feel that she already knew what I wanted to say. I was finally ready to say my prayer.

My Blessed Mother, the agony of loneliness breaks my heart. I know that this is not my life, this is not my destiny. I know my soul mate is here is this world, waiting for me as I am waiting for him. Please, I beg you to help him find me. Help him find his way home to me. Please, I beg you, help my husband find me. I can feel it: he's a typical man, lost and too proud to ask for directions. He just needs a little help. When he finds me, I promise you, we will bring our first child back to you. We will bring our child here, present the child to you, and baptize our child right here in your baptismal basin. We promise you.

I had wept all my tears. I was exhausted. There was nothing left. Done. As certain as I am of the air I breathe, our Virgin Mother was there with me. She held me and wiped away all my tears. I felt her presence, saw her face, and heard her voice. I was healed.

A new feeling came over me. Something I'd never quite felt before, something I'm not sure I even recognized. I stood there for a very long time, trying to understand what was happening. The only word in our language that comes close to describing the miracle that took place in my soul on that day is…surrender.

Not surrender in the sense of giving up; just the opposite. I surrendered completely to the Lord. I surrendered with absolute certainty that I was unconditionally loved, protected, and blessed by the Holy Spirit. I was a child of the divine light. I had surrendered to the Lord. Surrender—the act of knowing with absolute certainty that, no matter what happened, the light of the Lord was in my life and guiding my path.

Calm, peace, and serenity washed over me.

We live in an over-stimulated society in which we've come to expect everything to be larger than life. If someone says she has experienced a miracle, most of us expect to hear a larger-than-life story with a grand finale.

As I stood in front of the icon of the Virgin Mary that afternoon, I experienced a miracle. On the surface, it appeared that a woman had walked into a church, said a prayer, and left less than an hour later. That's not what happened. What really happened was that a woman's life was spiritually healed. By forgiving, I had won the greatest war ever waged against me, and by surrendering, I had opened the door to let God in, *unconditionally*.

The door of the church cracked open, and the lovely lady came back in to check on me.

"The priest will be available in a few minutes to offer a quick service."

My heart lit up. "Thank you."

"Before he gets here, would you like to see the Upper Room, where the Lord held the Last Supper?"

I couldn't believe it. I'd almost forgotten.

In the back of the church was a set of stone stairs, almost hidden. I said a quick prayer of thanks as the lady led me down the narrow stone stairs. The 'Upper Room' was actually down below. I caught my breath in awe of being there. It was such a small and simple room.

I had brief flashbacks of my trip to Rome many years before. I had spent hours gazing at Leonardo da Vinci's "The Last Supper." Clearly, Leonardo had never traveled to Jerusalem or stood in the Upper Room at Saint Mark's. This was where the Lord held his Last Supper. There were no windows here. It was just a plain and simple room.

Every Sunday of my life since, when I hear the priest bless the bread and wine in preparation of the Eucharist, I go back there. In my imagination, I stand again in the Upper Room.

After a few more moments of solitude and quiet prayer, I went back upstairs. The priest came and gave me the gift of a short service.

"Destiny, I failed you once, but today the door is wide open and I am here. I am ready to walk through. I don't know where you will lead me or what your plans for me are, but I am finally ready to walk through this door. Thank you for giving me a second chance." Gratitude filled my heart.

Chapter 14

The Call

On Sunday mornings, I loved to read the newspaper at Starbucks in Mizner Park. Mizner Park was why I moved to Boca. It was my favorite spot. I had been in south Florida for about a year and half, and I still loved it.

The move had been made possible by a huge career leap that shifted my career from marketing to sales. Being in sales meant I could travel, meet lots of people, make presentations, and actually see a bottom-line number with results. Sales is very different from marketing. Marketing is difficult to measure; sales are concrete and simple. Did you or did you not make your goal? I loved the simplicity. With this role came an awesome manager who told me I could live anywhere in the country as long as I had access to a major airport.

While still in New York, I traveled on weekends to explore my options and figure out where I wanted to live. First, I went to Boston, which is a great city, but the day I arrived was cold and rainy and that wasn't a good sign. Next, I explored Washington DC, which I've always loved, but couldn't find a great apartment within my price range. I headed south to Charleston, South Carolina. I had always found the South incredibly charming. I fell in love with Charleston and was serious about putting the city at the top of my list except that it lacked a major international airport. I would be doing a lot of traveling to Europe and required easy access to direct flights.

Continuing my journey, I flew to south Florida to visit with my sister Tina and her husband, who lived in the small town of Coconut Creek and promised to show me around. The day I arrived at Fort Lauderdale International Airport, my spirit blossomed. A huge smile swept across my face. There was something about being there that was uplifting, and I immediately knew I had found my new home. I love Florida—the sunshine, the beaches, the palm trees, and the insanely beautiful weather. I only needed to decide where in Florida I wanted to live.

Tina drove me up and down the east coast, from Miami all the way up to Jupiter. We explored every little town and neighborhood. One afternoon, we took a break to stop at a Starbucks for an afternoon latte.

When I walked into Mizner Park for the first time, I fell in love. Mizner Park is an outdoor shopping pavilion with upscale restaurants, cafes, shops, a movie theatre, and an art museum with an outdoor amphitheatre. As far as the eye could see, the streets were lined with tall, perfectly symmetrical palm trees and several soothing water fountains. Having grown up in New Jersey and lived in New York for most of my adult life, I had never imagined anyone lived like this—unless they were retired. It was very serene and peaceful.

For several months, I'd only considered moving to a big city and living in a tiny apartment, just because that's what people my age did. Thirty-year-olds with options did not move to Florida. Florida is where people came to retire. Then I thought, why not? I love it and it's beautiful.

Tina and I got our lattes at Starbucks and sat down at an outdoor table, taking a few quiet moments to enjoy the beautiful, sunny, south Florida morning. I finally asked, "Where are we?"

"We're in Mizner Park."

"I know that, but what town is this? Where are we in relation to the other towns we've driven to today."

"This is Boca Raton. Boca is the halfway point between Fort Lauderdale and West Palm Beach."

This was it. My heart knew that this was the place. "This is where I'm going to live. I'm moving here."

"Are you kidding? Jackie, everyone in Boca is retired. This is not where young, single people move. You should consider Miami or Fort Lauderdale, but definitely not Boca."

"No, this is it." I had made up my mind.

I found a realtor just a few blocks away from Mizner Park and told her I was looking for an adorable, two-bedroom place that was close to the beach, and

I wanted to move within the next two weeks. She quickly found several listings. The next day, I did a walkthrough of an amazing condo. It was huge: two bedrooms, two thousand square feet, a wraparound balcony, a golf course view, a mile from the beach, a luxury master bedroom with a Jacuzzi bath—and it was *less* than my current rent. I was stunned. I would have had to be a hedge fund manager to afford a place like this in New York City. It seemed too good to be true. How could it be so affordable? I didn't care. I loved it and signed a lease right away.

Two weeks later, I gave up my New Yorker status and moved to Boca Raton. The day I moved in, I noticed two hospice cars in the parking lot. I also met a few of my neighbors, and they were easily in their eighties. It took me all of two days to realize that I was the only thirty-year-old Christian girl living in a Jewish, Boca Raton retirement community. I was younger than the grandchildren of most of my neighbors. That explained my affordable rent.

I was amused. How had I ended up there? Maybe the Lord was trying to remind me that he has a great sense of humor. I loved the place. And, guess what? All my neighbors fell in love with me. They were the sweetest group of neighbors I had ever had. I became the biggest topic of conversation, and every little old lady there mothered me. Every time I traveled, went out, or had friends over, I got a barrage of questions. Strangely, I didn't mind the intrusion on my privacy. It made me feel safe, cared about, and loved. It was exactly what I needed.

That's how I ended up there in Boca Raton. My Sunday mornings in Mizner Park, drinking coffee and reading the paper became my favorite tradition. I worked very hard all week, and for the past year, in particular, I had practically lived on an airplane. My reward for this hard work was spending time in Mizner Park.

That Sunday felt a little bit heavy. I had a tremendously challenging week ahead of me. Five days of back-to-back meetings, important deadlines on deliverables I'd been preparing for months, and a forecast of zero downtime. It was the kind of week when what needs to be done is so stressful it almost chokes you. I would certainly need to work all that day. As soon as I finished my coffee, I would have to go back home and spend the rest of my Sunday on the computer in my home office, getting a head start on the week ahead.

My phone rang, interrupting my morning routine. It was Mom.

"Hi, Momma," I answered. I got up and started to make my way to one of the fountains. "I'm at Starbucks, having coffee."

We chatted for ten minutes about our week, updates on the families, and just catching up. I could tell there was something on her mind. I wasn't sure if it was good or bad, but she definitely had a peculiar edge to her voice.

"Momma, is there something you want to tell me," I wondered out loud.

In a very serious voice, she announced, "Jackie, last night I had a dream."

That's all it took. I knew this was serious. My family didn't share dreams often with each other. We all instinctively knew that dreams were sacred and to be shared only under very special circumstances. In fact, the only other dream my mother has ever shared with me was the one she had of the Virgin Mary the night before I was born. That was over thirty years before. For her to say the words, "I had a dream," was a very big deal.

"Tell me about it."

I could hear her take in a long, deep breath. I could almost hear her thinking, taking the time to slowly find the right words.

"Jackie, last night I dreamed of the Virgin Mary."

My heart skipped a beat. I wasn't expecting that. I quickly calculated in my head: exactly five weeks ago that day, I was standing in Jerusalem, praying in front of the icon of the Virgin Mary. I had not told anyone what happened to me that day or about my prayer. I had never spoken to anyone about how that afternoon changed my life forever.

My stomach suddenly knotted up in anticipation of what Mom would say next. There was silence on the phone. It was as if she knew that I needed a few moments to digest these words and prepare myself to hear what she had to say.

"Okay," I finally acknowledged.

"In my dream, the Virgin came to me and simply said, 'I'm ready to answer Jackie's prayer.'"

Just like that, a fountain of silent tears rolled down my face. My heart was racing, and my hand started to shake. Could it really be possible? I know I have

Certainty, but could it really be possible? I must have been silent too long. "Jackie. Jackie, are you still there?"

"Yes, Momma, I'm here," I managed to say, trying to muffle my tears.

"What does the dream mean? What did you pray?" she asked.

I didn't know how to answer her. I wasn't ready to tell anyone about my experience in Jerusalem. All I said was, "Momma, I know what she means."

My mother understood. She had perfect timing and knew when to probe and when to let go.

"I just wanted you to know…whatever you prayed for that day in our church…she came to me last night to let me know your prayer is ready to be answered."

"Thank you, Momma." I choked up. Momma knew the message that had been delivered through her was special.

I sat by myself on the edge of the fountain for over an hour. I reflected on the trip to Jerusalem, on my prayer, and on how much I had changed since that day. I was not the same person. Five weeks ago to that very day, I had surrendered my life to the Lord. I had given up any expectations of what I thought my life should look like and unconditionally accepted the journey the Lord had planned for me.

It had not been an easy task. It had been very hard to stop wanting specific results in my life. When I left Saint Mark's that day, the act of surrender had changed how I viewed the world and my role in it. I had let go of all my preconceived ideas of what my life should look like.

Since then, when I prayed, I didn't ask for anything specific. I only asked forgiveness for my sins and guidance on my life's purpose, and of course, I always offered thanks for my blessings. Most important, when I prayed, my focus was on others: family, friends, and communities on my prayer list.

A great spiritual teacher once taught me, "We are not allowed to witness anything in life unless we have also been given the ability to do something about it." I thought about this all the time. When I read the paper or heard about some challenge or tragedy, I always asked myself what I could do about the situation and why I had been allowed to witness it. Some situations do call for action, but sometimes the most important thing I could do was simply pray. And so, my prayer list grew every day.

Since I had returned from Jerusalem, my days had been like a roller coaster ride. My emotions were running all over the place, I had an insane work schedule, and, frankly, I had been way too busy to sit down and reflect. My crazy schedule had taken over. Until Mom's call. The call froze time, and the swirl around me seemed to move in slow motion. For the first time since Jerusalem, I took time to stop and reflect.

She was ready to answer my Prayer. The Virgin Mary had come to Mom and told her she was ready to answer my Prayer. I reminded myself to take a deep breath, relax, and offer thanks.

Thank you, Lord. Thank you, Jesus. And thank you to our Blessed Virgin Mary. Thank you, Certainty. Thank you with every ounce of my being and my soul.

Chapter 15

Destiny

As soon as I got in the car, I almost changed my mind. I was exhausted. It had been a long week and, quite frankly, I was not in the mood for a party. Still, I had to go. I'd just say hello to Todd and leave early, I decided. I fumbled around in the dim light, looking for the directions. I had gone to Fort Lauderdale only a handful of times, and I still wasn't sure how to get downtown.

Todd and I had known each other for years. He was the friend from Long Island who had organized the dismal raft-up that made me decide to leave New York. He was one of the most sociable and fun people you'd ever meet. Once you get on his email list, you're a friend for life. That's how he is. Todd was one of the last people I said goodbye to when I moved to Boca.

The previous Tuesday night, he had called. In his classic, larger-than-life style, he said he knew a guy who had a house in Fort Lauderdale, and he and a big group of friends from Long Island were flying down to stay there for the upcoming boat show. They were throwing a huge party on Saturday night, and I just had to be there.

I was not in the mood even early in the week. I was working long hours at the time, and I was mentally drained. I also didn't look forward to partying with a bunch of single guys from Long Island. If it had been anyone else but Todd, I would have politely declined, but we hadn't seen each other in over a year and a half.

Reluctantly, I accepted, but I added one little white lie. I told Todd I had a boyfriend. The last thing I wanted was for any guy at this party to think I was single. I did not want to get hit on by any out-of-state guys on vacation. I'd just make a quick appearance and get home early, I told myself.

I pulled up to the house a little after dark. It was a spectacular, newly constructed mansion on the intercoastal in the Las Olas Isles of Fort Lauderdale. The home was impressive and stately, surrounded by stunning landscaping tall palm trees and a gated entrance. Although the house was huge, it looked quite warm and inviting, as well.

Suddenly, something odd hit me. There didn't seem to be a party. In fact, hardly any cars were parked on the street. I double checked the address and checked the number on the gate. Yes, it was the right house. Was I too early?

Flashbacks of the cancelled raft-up went through my mind. The last time I got an invitation from Todd for a supposedly huge event, it turned out to be a small disaster. I swore that if Todd had invited me to this house and there was no party, he was going to owe me big time.

As I started toward the gate, my doubts took over. What was I doing there? I couldn't hear any music. I considered turning around and getting back in my car, but just then, someone on a Harley parked next to my car. He spotted me right away and made his way towards me. I thought I would look foolish if I turned around and got back in my car.

The tall man from the Harley approached. "Hi, I'm Joe."

"Hi, Joe, I'm Jackie."

"Hey, Jackie. So, how do you know Chris?"

"I don't know Chris. My friend Todd invited me."

"Oh. I have no idea who Todd is."

I was starting to feel a bit awkward, but there was no turning back by then, so Joe and I walked in together. From a grand center hall foyer, we stepped down into a sunken living room accented by a vaulted ceiling and twenty-foot floor-to-ceiling glass windows.

The first thing I noticed was the angel above the fireplace. It was a stunning, hand-carved, six-foot-tall wooden angel with a four-foot wingspan. I stood there staring at it, mesmerized. He was beautiful. For a moment, I completely forgot where I was or how I got there.

I began to notice my surroundings. This was not the house of a bachelor, as I had assumed. It was definitely a family home. Family photos were everywhere, adults and children covering every wall and counter. In the foyer, an ornate antique Bible and a pile of rosaries graced a coffee table. Crosses and religious pictures adorned every wall. I could see that this home had been decorated by a mother, a woman of faith. It was a gracious and welcoming home.

The moment we walked in, Joe had left my side and slipped through the sliding glass doors leading to the back deck. Obviously, he'd been there before and knew the house well. I'm not sure how long I stood there, taking in my surroundings.

I quickly realized there was, in fact, no party. I was standing in a stranger's home, completely alone. No crowds, no music, and definitely no party. Once again, I contemplated discreetly leaving. Then I heard a voice that seemed to be addressing me.

"Hey, there. I'm Carlos. How do you know Chris?"

I followed the voice and walked through a breakfast room to get within view of whoever was talking to me. The voice had come from the kitchen. A casually dressed guy was seated at the island, enjoying his dinner, and I guess he had noticed me standing by myself in the living room. I probably looked ridiculous just standing there, staring at the angel.

"Hi, Carlos. I'm Jackie. I don't know Chris. I was invited by my friend Todd."

"Who the hell is Todd?" Carlos blurted out.

At that point, I definitely felt like I had just crashed someone's home. What was I doing there? Nothing about this made any sense. Why had Todd invited me to that house? Why had he told me there would be a party there that night? Why didn't anyone there know who he was?

I needed to leave, and by then I didn't care whether anyone saw me walk out the front door with no explanation. However, as I made my way back through the breakfast room and across the living room, I was intercepted.

A dark-haired man in blue swim trunks barreled through the sliding glass doors into the living room. He didn't have a shirt on, just a towel wrapped around his shoulders. He was soaking wet, obviously just out of the pool. Oh my goodness, but he was cute! He was also half-naked and smiling at me—and that smile was melting me.

Full of excitement and exuberance, he put his hand out to shake mine and announced, "Hi, I'm Chris."

So, I had finally met this Chris that everyone had been mentioning since I got there. "Hi, I'm Jackie. I think I just crashed your house or your party, or… I'm not sure. Either way, I'm not sure what I'm doing here. Um, Todd invited me, but I don't know where he is. He said there was a party here tonight. Um, he invited me. Um, I don't know where he is."

What had I just said? I wondered. I was mumbling. What was wrong with me? I sounded like an idiot. Why was I mumbling? What had happened to the confident me? I was extremely nervous. Why was I suddenly so nervous and unable to speak clearly? The whole thing was weird. I realized I was smiling and I wondered why. Had he noticed how stupid I sounded? He was cute, really cute. Oh, my goodness.

A hot, half-naked man was standing in front of me, and I sounded like a total idiot. I ordered myself to pull it together. Please, please, I implored myself, don't say anything stupid. Play it cool and stop mumbling.

"Oh, yeah. The party was last night. We're all exhausted, so tonight we decided to just hang out and throw something on the grill. Todd is outside. I think he's in the pool."

Something about the moment felt surreal. I was standing in a complete stranger's living room, and a six-foot-tall angel was perched over the fireplace, staring down at us. A really cute guy that I had just met was standing in front of me, half naked and dripping water all over the floor. I was so nervous and so afraid of saying anything stupid that I probably paused for longer than I should have before replying.

"Um...the party was *last* night?"

I hadn't meant to say that. I really did sound stupid. Why was I so nervous around this guy?

Please, Lord, I'm begging you right now, please stop me from saying anything else that sounds stupid.

He had a very warm smile and I couldn't get over how cute he was. He had dark brown eyes, a perfect nose, and really great teeth. And, despite my nervousness, I could tell he liked me, too.

"Yeah, but don't worry about that. Stay. Hang out. We have a ton of food on the grill. Carlos has his yacht parked behind the house, and we all might go out for a late night cruise later. Are you hungry? The food should be ready in about ten minutes. We have steak, chicken, corn, burgers—anything you want, just name it. Oh, and drinks. We have lots of drinks, too. Yes, we have drinks."

Finally, I laughed and started to relax. He was mumbling, too. He was just as nervous as I was. A huge smile swept across my face. In fact, it was the first time in over a week that I felt I could relax.

Chris and I spent the next hour chatting away. It was the nervous, get-to-know-you small talk between two people who obviously like each other. I learned that the house belonged to his parents and he was down there for a long weekend to attend the boat show, an annual tradition.

Chris lived in Long Island, where he had his own company. I must admit, upon hearing that, my heart broke a little. Doubt invaded my brain and warned me not to fall for a guy who lived in New York. It had taken me a decade to escape from New York, and I had no desire to go back, ever. But every time Doubt invaded my thoughts, I told him to shut up. This guy was really cute.

Chris was single and had a seven-year-old daughter. He beamed with excitement every time he spoke about her, and I immediately knew he was an amazing father. His other passion and love in life was the U.S. Coast Guard. He had joined the Coast Guard Auxiliary shortly after September 11th. It was a poignant and sensitive subject for him. Months later, I would learn how much Chris had lost following that event. Unlike me, who had wallowed in self-pity for years, he had emerged as one of the heroes with a burning desire to serve others.

He spoke fast and mumbled a lot. I immediately sensed he liked me as much as I liked him. We were both very nervous. We learned quite a lot about each other in those first few hours, but at the same time, I felt I already "knew" him. It was very strange. I had never felt this kind of instant connection with anyone.

We enjoyed a feast for dinner. There were about a dozen people at the house. It was not exactly a party, but as the night grew, quite a few people came in and out. Eventually, I connected with Todd. He immediately caught onto the fact that Chris and I had been talking all evening and were attracted to each other. Todd made it clear to me that he did not approve.

Of course, my dilemma was that I liked this guy a lot, but earlier in the week I had lied to Todd when I said I had a boyfriend. So, Todd thought I was playing games with his friend. I wondered how to handle such a situation.

Well, it would have been best if I had not lied to Todd in the first place, but it was too late for that, so my strategy for the night was to avoid and ignore Todd. I knew it was an immature and rude strategy, especially since he was a good friend, but in my defense, have I mentioned how cute this guy was? I really liked him. Whatever this was, I had never felt it before. So, there you have it. I spent the night hanging out with Chris, and I avoided Todd. However, I did say a quick prayer in front of the angel, asking him to forgive me for my pre-meditated rudeness.

The crowd dispersed. A few people were out in the back by the pool and another group was in the home theatre, watching a movie. Chris and I were alone in the kitchen. He told me about his parents' charitable foundation, which they had started over a decade before. It was dedicated to the education of seminarians and to supporting the Rosa Mystica House of Prayer in Edmeston, New York.

I wasn't sure why he was telling me so much. I'd only met him a few hours before, and we were having a very deep conversation for two people who had just met. Chris didn't even know my religious views. Nonetheless, I felt deeply connected to him.

Suddenly, I did something very spontaneous. I have no idea where I got the courage. Certainty must have stepped in and taken over. In my handbag, I carried a wallet-sized photo of the icon of the Virgin Mary from Jerusalem. I had only two of these photos, and they meant everything in the world to me—literally. Those two photos were my most treasured possessions. I took one of the photos out.

"Chris, I have no idea why I'm doing this, but there is some voice in my head that's telling me it's the right thing to do," I explained as I handed him the photo. "I want you to have this. It's the sacred icon of the Virgin Mary from Jerusalem. She is located in the Church of the Upper Room, where the Last Supper was held. It's very special to me."

I paused and took a deep breath. Then, I said again with Certainty, "I want you to have this."

Chris looked at the picture, smiled, and said, "You're not going to believe this."

"Oh, try me," I thought but did not say out loud.

"I've seen this picture before."

I was taken aback. "How? This is very rare. This is not exactly a famous portrait."

"I've seen this picture. This same picture is hanging in my parent's home up in Long Island."

I was speechless.

Chapter 16

My Miracle

It was getting late. Chris and I walked out to the pool and sat on a long chaise lounge. My head was spinning. I'd never felt this way about anyone. Ever.

Was this real? Was my mind playing games with me? Should I play it safe and not get caught up in the moment? I thought about the angel. How often does someone walk into a house where a six-foot-tall angel watches over you? That had to mean something. Also, Chris had a connection to the portrait of the icon, didn't that have to mean something, too? Were these all signs, or was I making too much of them? I wondered what Chris was thinking.

I thought about Mom's call the Sunday before and her dream. The Virgin Mary had come to her and said that she was ready to answer my prayer. Could Chris possibly be the answer to my prayer? My mind was whirling. I didn't know what to think or believe, and I didn't want to fabricate something in my head that wasn't real. I needed a sign, something clear-cut that would leave no room for confusion. If this man was the answer to my prayer, I wanted concrete proof.

I must have been lost in my thoughts for a little too long. Suddenly very serious, Chris interrupted my thoughts. "I want to share something with you."

"Sure, go ahead."

For the first time that night, he wasn't mumbling or talking too fast.

"Before I flew down here, I got a call from my mother."

I wondered where this was going.

"Remember, I told you about my family's foundation and the church the foundation rebuilt in upstate New York? Well, we have a spiritual director up there who receives messages from the Blessed Mother. I know it may sound hard to believe, but I really do believe these messages are, in fact, very special."

I was still amazed that I had met a guy from such a spiritual family, one that had an unusually strong connection to the Virgin Mary. I had no idea where he was going with his story, but I could clearly see that he was tense.

"Well, my mom got a call from the spiritual director this past Sunday."

The past Sunday? My mother called me that same Sunday about her dream.

Chris looked deep into my eyes, locked into my gaze, and said, "It was a message for me:

'Before Chris leaves on his trip, tell him to offer a prayer of thanks to the Blessed Mother. She has a miracle waiting for him.'"

My heart stopped. I stopped breathing. Everything in time ceased. I was frozen. I had no idea what to say. Yes, I know, I'm not being rational. Of course, I was still breathing, and my heart didn't actually stop, but my universe had been rocked.

How do I describe the moment of a miracle? How do I explain with words, which are so limiting, something so unexplainable? All I could think was whether this was really happening. Was it really happening?

"When I first got the message," Chris continued, "I thought it must have to do with business, because I was scheduled to meet a few investors while I was down here."

Long pause. I reminded myself to breathe, to listen, and remember to breathe.

"But now, I think it was about us. I think this—what we have here—this is the miracle that was waiting for me."

Time stood still. I used every ounce of reasoning ability I had left in my brain to memorize that moment, to capture it, and to remember it forever. That was the first moment of the rest of my life.

It was also the longest time all evening that I remained silent. I couldn't speak. I was awestruck. Eventually, I caught onto the fact that my silence was making Chris nervous. He had just shared something extremely personal and profound, and I had suddenly gone mute. It was time to break the silence.

"I'd like to share something with you."

Now it was his turn to sit back intently and listen.

"I just got back five weeks ago…oh, well, six weeks ago now…from a trip to Jerusalem."

I stopped, wondering whether I should continue. Was I really going to tell him my story? I hadn't shared it with anyone in the world, and I had met him only a few hours before. I called on Certainty to let me know if I should continue. Certainty found his way into my heart and let me know it was safe to tell him.

"During my trip, I prayed in front of the icon of the Virgin Mary."

"That's the photo you gave me earlier tonight?"

"Yes." I was getting very nervous. I wasn't sure how to continue. Should I tell him everything? Should I filter it? The words came forth. "I've never told anyone what I prayed for that day. Anyway, I got a call from my mom this past Sunday, too. She had a dream of the Virgin Mary with a message for me. The message was that she was ready to answer my prayer."

Chris interrupted, "Are you saying that both of our mothers got messages this past Sunday from the Blessed Mother?"

I tried to lighten up the moment a little. "Yeah. Do you think it's a coincidence?"

"Probably not." Chris offered me a huge smile. We were both on the same page. "Are you going to tell me what you prayed for?" he asked.

With absolute certainty and for the first time, I told someone else about my prayer. "I prayed that my soul mate would find me."

I remembered to take a deep breath, to keep breathing, to relax. We shared a long, intimate gaze as we both processed the moment. We had only known each other for a few hours, and it didn't seem possible. How was it possible to know with certainty that you've finally met the person you're going to spend the rest of your life with after only a few hours?

I guess the moment got a little too intense, because Chris broke the silence in a somewhat joking manner. "So, I guess you're my miracle, and I'm the answer to your prayer."

"I guess so."

"I think this would be a good time to ask if you would like to go out to dinner with me tomorrow night?"

The following night Chris took me to Mangos, a chic restaurant on downtown Fort Lauderdale's Las Olas Boulevard. I was very nervous, yet at the same time I had never felt more comfortable and safe around anyone. I knew I was finally home.

During dinner, we shared stories, we laughed, we told jokes, and we got lost in each other. Certainty whispered in my ear: "You two have known each other for lifetimes, so just have fun tonight and get re-acquainted." My face ached from smiling so much. I had never been happier in my life.

After dinner, we took a stroll down Las Olas Boulevard. It was a beautiful, crisp night. As we walked hand-in-hand past all the fancy shops, listening to the bustle of crowds around us, I knew everything was perfect. I was memorizing the moment. It is a rare, special gift when you know you're living a perfect moment.

During our stroll, with every step we took and every story we told and every laugh we shared, I was falling in love. I was falling in love.

As we rounded the corner of a quiet block, Chris stopped me, took me in his arms, looked deep into eyes, and we shared our first kiss. The world I was living in was perfect, and this was the most perfect first kiss ever invented, since the beginning of time. Little could I imagine how much that moment would change my life.

He looked deep in my eyes for what seemed like an eternity. The illusion of it being just a first date was just that—it was an illusion. Certainty was right, we had known each other for lifetimes.

Chris broke the magical silence by announcing, "I'm going to marry you."

I jokingly responded, "Are you sure?"

"I've never been more certain of anything in my life." Just like that, we were engaged.

My prayer *was* answered.

Chapter 17

Engaged

Exactly two weeks to the day after Chris and I met, I flew up to New York. We had an appointment with Father Darius of Saint Dominic's Roman Catholic Church in Oyster Bay, New York, to fill out our marriage application for the church.

I knew the date I wanted, and it was available. Everything was going smoothly until I noticed a delicate question on the marriage application. "How long have you known each other?" I must have stared at that question for at least five minutes. I had no idea how to answer it. If I told the truth, which was two weeks, would Father Darius refuse to marry us until much later? On the other hand, if I explained the entire story to him, told him about my trip to Israel, my mom's dream, Chris's mom's message from the Blessed Mother, and how this was meant to be, what would he think?

We had been instructed to fill out our own applications, so we couldn't exactly compare answers with Father Darius sitting there. But then, Father Darius was called to attend to something and excused himself.

I seized the moment. "Put three months for this question, and let's both say a few Hail Mary's and ask God to forgive us for lying on our marriage application."

"Jackie, we can't lie on our marriage application," Chris protested.

"It's not a big lie. It's a very small lie. Two weeks, three months—what's the difference?"

I was agonizing over one question. What if the Church thought we were not ready to get married? That was it. It was settled. "I'm putting three months. After we're married, I promise to go to confession and ask for forgiveness."

The moment I made this declaration, I instantly regretted it. I could almost hear Certainty screaming in my ear, "What are you doing? Did you forget about me? I thought you believed in me? Just tell the truth. How can you even consider anything else?"

Just as I was about to erase my answer, Father Darius came back in. We handed him our completed applications and waited. I had knots in my stomach. I was in agony. I couldn't believe I had just lied to the Church on my marriage application. Was it too late to confess? Father reviewed our application and brought up the three months. "It's not a very long time," he said.

Chris responded instantly. "Father, I knew within the first hour of our meeting that we were destined to be together."

Soon, everything was finalized, and we were on the calendar for the following June.

For the next few days, Certainty reprimanded me. "What did you do? You have to make this right. Go to confession." So I did. Not two days after completing my marriage application, I went to confession. The lie had been a powerful reminder of how cunning Doubt was becoming. The more I loved and embraced Certainty, the harder Doubt fought to sneak into my life. Sometimes, he got in through the cracks, and I had to sweep him back out.

Our next duty was to tell our families. Our engagement was still a "secret." No one in either of our families knew. We decided to wait for two months, until Christmas, before making the big announcement. We wanted to enjoy some privacy in our relationship for just a little while longer before adding our families into the equation.

In the meantime, we loved our secret engagement. We started planning the wedding immediately. I bought my wedding dress, and we booked the banquet hall. Most important, we began planning the details of our new life together.

About two weeks before Christmas, I flew back to New York to join Chris and his parents at their friends' annual Christmas party. The four of us drove to the party together. After parking the car, Chris pulled me aside and whispered in my ear, "I think we should tell them tonight." That was not the plan, and I quickly tried to stop him. "No, I'm not ready."

"It's perfect. It's a Christmas party and everyone is in great spirits." He was bursting with excitement.

Suddenly, I got very nervous. I was nervous enough about joining the family to meet their friends, and I just wasn't prepared to tell them, yet. So, as we stood on the steps of the beautifully decorated home full of Christmas lights, nativity scenes, and mistletoe, Chris spontaneously announced, "Oh, Mom, Dad, by the way, Jackie and I wanted to let you know we're getting married."

His mom, Noreen, quickly chimed in. "Yes, we know. In June. We bumped into Father Darius and he congratulated us. We were waiting to see how long it would take you two to let us in on the big announcement."

I guess the surprise was on us!

"Don't worry," she went on. "We haven't told anyone else. We figured you kids had good reason to keep this to yourselves for a while. Anyway, we love you both, and congratulations," Noreen said as she kissed us both on the cheek.

"Congratulations, kids," said Joe, Chris's dad. "Oh, and by the way, Abbey also told us indirectly."

Now, we were both shocked. Noreen explained. "Yes, if it hadn't been for Father Darius, I think we would have been a little suspicious anyway when Abbey told us about your trip to New York City and Jackie buying a beautiful wedding dress. Seven-year-olds love sharing such colorful details."

How could we have been so foolish? We actually thought it would be a surprise. I started laughing, and my nervousness disappeared. In the future, we would have to work a little harder to keep our secrets.

We walked in the door, wishing everyone a Merry Christmas, and for the first time, Chris proudly introduced me to everyone as his finance. What a magical night!

The following week, Chris flew back down to Florida to have an early Christmas dinner with my family and to ask my father's permission for my hand in marriage. I'd never seen him so nervous. He was shaking when he delivered his speech to my dad, telling him how much he loved me and wanted the honor of marrying me. Dad was amused at his formality. "Yes, you can have her," he joked, "but there is a no return policy."

We were openly engaged, we had a wedding date, I had a dress, and the banquet hall had been booked. Only one tiny little detail was still missing. Chris had never officially proposed to me. On the night of our first date, he had told me he was going to marry me, and we both just knew. Even so, I was expecting a formal proposal.

Just a week after we had met, for our second date, Chris stole a scene from a Hollywood movie. I had no idea where we were going or what he had planned for the day. He drove us to the Boca Town Center Mall. At first, I thought it was interesting that he wanted to spend our second date shopping at the mall, but he knew I was a former Jersey Girl and actually do love malls. He was wearing a peculiar grin and was brimming with anticipation. As we strolled through the mall, Chris walked me right into Tiffany's. Immediately, we were led to a private table in the back. "I made an appointment for us. Pick out any ring you want," he announced.

"Are you serious?" was my stunned reaction.

"Yes. I want you to pick something you love." He was smiling broadly. I'm not sure who was enjoying the moment more.

"Okay, then," I said, and I focused my attention on the jeweler. "Please show me the largest and most expensive rock you have." I was joking, of course. I turned around to Chris and said seriously, "I appreciate this beautiful gesture very much, but you do realize this isn't important to me? I'm not a girl who measures her life by such things. I don't need a diamond ring from Tiffany's to know that my prayer has been answered."

"I know, and that's why I love you and why I'm going to marry you. I still want you to have a beautiful ring that you love. Go ahead and pick something out."

Only one week before, exactly, I had been single and my favorite stop at the Boca Town Center Mall was Teavana. My one simple luxury was a fresh-brewed custom tea served with rock cane sugar. Now, I was in Tiffany's, picking out my engagement ring. More important, I was standing next to the man who made my heart sing. It was surreal how fast everything was happening. How had I ended up there? Was I dreaming?

Certainty found his way into my heart and whispered, "God does not need months or years to manifest a miracle. When you are ready, He is ready."

I reminded myself of those words every single day. "When you are ready, He is ready." Life doesn't have to be a long, arduous journey full of twists and turns. I became ready when I surrendered. It was just that simple.

After we both picked out the ring, Chris told me, "I'm not ready to give this to you. I want to surprise you with a special engagement night." And that's how I knew that a special engagement night and a formal proposal were coming.

Three days before Christmas, we enjoyed a quiet dinner at a very private and romantic restaurant in Boca Raton. Chris reserved a booth in the back room, and a huge bouquet of roses was waiting for me at our table. For some reason, despite the flowers and romantic restaurant, I was not suspicious that the night was anything other than a romantic date.

Seated in front of us was a gentleman celebrating his eightieth birthday, surrounded by eight women in their fifties. They were a loud, joyous group, and I found it amusing to observe them. The man certainly looked like he was enjoying life.

Our waiter came and opened a beautiful bottle of champagne. We toasted to a wonderful night, the magic of the Christmas season, and then we toasted again to wish the gentleman sitting next to us a happy birthday. On a normal night, I imagine this restaurant was quiet and intimate, but not that night. The birthday group was celebrating like it was New Years Eve.

So much was I enjoying the revelry that I missed the signs that Chris wasn't quite himself.

For a lovely surprise, a violinist came to our table and played exclusively for us. I enjoyed the moment but didn't imagine it was a prelude to more. I was lost in the music when Chris took my hand and asked, "Do you want to dance?"

"No, no," I said quickly, "not in front of all these people."

"Please, let's get up and dance," he insisted.

I had no idea what was going on. "No, I don't want to get up in front of all these people and be the only ones dancing. Let's just enjoy the music."

Chris resorted to begging, "Please, please, let's get up and dance."

I heard the anxiousness in his voice and wondered about it. Reluctantly, I stood up. He took my hand. I noticed he was shaking. The violinist stepped back and stopped playing, and everyone in the restaurant got very quiet. All the revelry, music, and chatter stopped. There was silence. All eyes were on us.

An old woman from the back of the restaurant broke the silence with a scream. "Oh, my God, he's going to propose!" Patrons stopped eating, waiters stopped serving, and the bartender stopped mixing drinks. All eyes were on us.

I finally understood what was going on. Poor Chris was shaking, he was so nervous. I wasn't sure he could propose with everyone staring at him.

He took a small box out of his pocket and was about to hand it to me when a woman from the birthday party yelled, "Hey, son, don't just hand it to her. Get down on one knee!"

Another woman joined in from another corner of the restaurant. "Yeah, get down on your knee. That's how you do it." A third woman interjected, "Now, say something romantic, and loud enough for all of us to hear."

Poor Chris, I'm sure he had not been planning on receiving step-by-step instructions, and he was suffering from serious stage fright. Nervously, he dropped to one knee, quickly opened the box, and blurted out, "I love you. Will you marry me?" I was in tears.

The ladies started yelling, "Well, honey, what do you say?" "Did she say yes?" "Show us that ring!"

"Yes," I announced, loud enough for all to hear, as I held out my hand and displayed the ring. Applause and cheers erupted. Well-wishers came over to our table for the rest of the evening, offering congratulations and sharing their own engagement stories. I was surprised and elated. It was also funny. Poor Chris had had no idea his perfectly planned romantic proposal would get hijacked by the older ladies in the restaurant.

Here is a lesson to all future gentlemen who may consider proposing to their girlfriends on a Saturday night in Boca Raton. The women of Boca are not shy about contributing to your perfectly planned proposal. As for me, I loved it. It was the most perfect proposal in the world.

We had been engaged for two months, but the proposal night was the most beautiful night of my life. I was in heaven.

Chapter 18

Coming Back

It was cold, mind-numbing cold. The dashboard showed the outside temperature was five degrees. With the wind-chill factor, I'm sure it must have been ten below. Even with the heat on, we were freezing inside the car. A light snow was falling, and the windshield wipers swiped back and forth, keeping our view clear.

Chris had warned me it would be a long trip, especially in this kind of weather, but I had not expected so much snow. We raced against time. The snow was coming down heavier by the minute, slowing us down. The roads might soon become treacherous. We had to find a balance between reaching our destination before the snow got worse and driving slowly enough to stay safe. An accident where we were in upstate New York was not an option. I had not seen a bar on my cell phone in over an hour. We easily had another hour or more of driving in these conditions. My fingers were numb.

Bailey didn't mind the drive. He was happily snuggled up in his new wool-lined carrier. I couldn't help turning around every five minutes to check on him. My maternal instincts were in high gear.

Right after the New Year, Chris had asked me what I wanted for Valentine's Day.

I knew the answer immediately. "I want a puppy."

"Anything else? How about jewelry, a trip, concert tickets, anything else?"

"No, I want a puppy."

I had always dreamed of having a puppy. We had one as kids, but briefly. My uncle Mike bought a mixed-breed puppy as a Christmas present for my brother Christian. He was small and playful, and we all fell in love with him. Although he was technically my brother's dog, he had three older sisters, and we got to name him. We chose Cupcake. The dog was male, but we still thought Cupcake was a perfect name. He quickly earned the nickname Cuppy.

Cuppy grew to over seventy pounds. Our greatest joy was jumping on his back and riding him like a pony. One day, Cuppy didn't feel well and Mom took him to the vet. When we came home from school, she told us that the vet loved him so much he wanted to keep him. The vet had a big farm upstate, she said, and Cuppy would be happier there. All of us cried and took our anger out on Mommy. We kept yelling at her, "How could you give our dog away?"

One night after my mom thought we were all sleeping, I sneaked into the kitchen and saw Mom looking at a picture of Cuppy. She was crying. I never understood how she could give him away if she loved him so much. I had no idea that Cuppy hadn't made it, and that the "big farm upstate" was really doggy heaven. It took me many years to realize that Mom made up the story to spare us. We all missed Cuppy.

I told Chris about Cuppy. Mom refused to bring another dog home. She said she couldn't handle another loss.

Hearing the story, Chris was trapped. "How can I deny you a puppy after hearing that?" In fairness, I will admit it was a dirty card to play, but I really wanted a puppy.

I found a flyer for a new litter of Shih Tzus from a breeder in Boca. I called the breeder. She had two puppies left, a male and a female, and she said we could come over anytime.

We arrived at a home in an upscale, gated community and were led to the back sunroom. Upon entering, I saw a tiny little pure-white puppy, tangled up in a ball of yarn. As soon as he saw me, this little guy ran over, jumped on my leg, and showered me with kisses. He was tiny, no more than two pounds, silky soft, and perfect. I couldn't let go of him. Chris watched this display and logically concluded, "I guess we're getting a puppy."

"Look, he chose us. He loves us. It was meant to be," I proudly declared. That was the moment I became a mom, a mom to my Bailey. It was my first glimpse of a new and different layer of happiness and joy.

The roads had turned icy, and the snow was coming down harder. We were only five miles from our destination. A week before, I was living among the palm trees in my dream apartment in Boca Raton, and now I was back in upstate New York.

Everything happened so fast: meeting Chris, the secret engagement, the official engagement, and now my decision to move back to New York sooner rather than later to plan the wedding and spend more time together. I found a temporary apartment for a few months until the June wedding. Chris helped me pack up my place in Boca, and we began the road trip from Florida back to New York.

I had never, ever, ever thought I'd be making this trip. I was leaving my personal paradise. It amazed me that I had left New York for Florida only to meet a New Yorker and return a year and a half later.

Sometimes, I wondered if God was looking down from heaven and enjoying a good laugh. I could almost hear Him whispering, "You needed the time off. The break from New York began the process of healing, but you have to go back, now. You still have more work to do up here. Remember, you surrendered control of your life to Me, and this is your path. Trust the process, especially now, when it's leading you right back to what you ran away from."

I was certain. My life with Chris was everything, and it meant we had to live in New York. I had flexibility in my career and could work from anywhere, but he needed to be up there. Despite having to move, I was happier than ever.

Our journey took three days. Our first stop was Hilton Head, South Carolina. The hotel would not allow us to check in with Bailey. I had got him a week before, and he was only eight weeks old. I absolutely would not leave him in a kennel.

Chris found a doggy hotel and spa nearby. Bailey's room cost about half as much as the Hilton. For this price, I was assured that someone on staff would give my puppy a massage, rub his paws, and play ball with him. Chris rolled his eyes at the sales pitch, but I didn't see it as absurd. Upon my insistence, Chris reluctantly agreed to check Bailey into the spa. I guess the true meaning of motherhood comes to you on the day you realize that you will forever be spending more money on your children—in this case my puppy—than you would ever spend on yourself.

The next stop was Washington, DC. I quickly concluded that a doggy spa in our nation's capital would set our budget back too much, so we snuck Bailey into our room. No, that was not my proudest moment. I know it was wrong. This was my second realization about motherhood: spending stupid amounts of money on your "children" wears out very quickly. I do love him, but Bailey didn't need a massage two days in a row.

We left Washington very early the following morning for the final leg of our journey to my apartment upstate. I was already feeling homesick. The minute our car drove past the Welcome-to-New-York sign, I turned to Chris. "You have to promise me one thing. Please, I beg you, as soon as we can, promise me we'll move back to Florida."

"I promise."

I couldn't see anything. The storm was in full force, and we had only about two feet of visibility. Everything was covered in snow.

I turned around to check on Bailey. He was sleeping, bundled up in his brand-new pink coat. The day before, we had stopped at Wal-Mart to buy Bailey a jacket. The only jacket left in x-small for a two-pound puppy was a Juicy Couture Pink Fur knock-off. Chris was horrified when he saw it, and I think Bailey was, too. I didn't care. At least he was warm.

It was very late at night when we finally arrived. Chris decided, "Let me get you both inside first, turn up the heat, and I'll unpack the car. We won't be able to go anywhere or see anything until this storm clears."

I took a moment to reflect on our journey. We had left four days before, had traveled through nine states, and had driven 1,382 miles. The day we left, it was seventy-one degrees in Boca and now it was two below. All I could say was, "Do you have any idea how much I love you?"

Chris could read my thoughts. "I know coming back was a huge sacrifice for you, but look at the bright side..." I waited. Chris finally continued, "Okay, I can't think of one right now, but something will come to me." I could. The bright side was that I had never loved anyone so much. The journey continually reminded me of our miracle, and I was willing to make any sacrifice in the world for us.

Chapter 19

Wedding Day

I often wonder about the idea of a miracle. Is it something you feel? Can you see it? Or is it something you just know? Miracle is a very big word, perhaps best saved for big events like the birth of a baby or the first man walking on the moon.

As I ponder this thought, I'm surrounded by lovely, fresh-cut flowers. Isn't the blossoming of these flowers a miracle? A tiny little seed in the ground, nurtured with rich soil, water, and light, grows to reveal its unique beauty. When we look at the seed, we can't see the miracle. It's only later, after its potential has been manifested, we realize what that seed carried all along. Isn't that how we all are? On the journey of our destiny in this life, all of us start as seeds. Some of us are still in the ground, waiting to grow. Some of us have sprouted a few leaves, and some of us have fully blossomed. Is the miracle the blossoming of the flower, or is the miracle knowing with certainty that everything is already in the seed? Yes, for me it always comes down to certainty. When all I can see is a seed in the ground, the miracle is certainty in my knowledge of what the seed is destined to become.

These were the thoughts I recorded in my journal on the morning of our wedding. I have heard that most brides wake up jittery and full of excitement, perhaps thinking about their hair and make-up, the excitement of the day ahead, and how the weather will hold up. I woke up and started writing.

> 'What is a miracle? Today I will get married. I will marry the man who makes my heart sing and who was sent as the answer to my prayer. A man who calls me his miracle. Today is our seed, the first day of our journey as husband and wife. We don't know how our seed will grow. We don't know how many leaves will bloom or what its flower will look like. We don't know what storms we'll face. We do know with certainty that this seed is our destiny. It is our miracle.'

We were all ready. The driver took my hand and escorted me to my seat in the limo. My heart was full of love and excitement. Joining me on the journey to the church were Mom and Dad, five bridesmaids, and one junior bridesmaid.

We were only a few miles from the church, and I wanted to use the time to relax and say my prayers. I was about to get married. I was quietly lost in my own thoughts when my sister Claudia interrupted me. "Jackie, how far away from the church are we?"

"About five or ten minutes, depending on traffic," I answered. "By my estimate, we should arrive at least ten minutes early."

"Okay. The only reason I ask is because we've been driving for twenty minutes now, and the driver just drove past the same restaurant twice."

I looked through the window and didn't recognize any of the streets. "What are you trying to say?" I started getting nervous.

"Jackie, this guy is totally lost. Someone has to say something."

All of us in the limo were from out of town and not familiar with the back streets of this tiny hamlet of Oyster Bay, New York. Come to think of it, I had no idea how to get to the church myself. I knew about how far it was, and I just assumed the limo driver would have directions and know where he was going. What kind of limo driver gets lost?

Claudia tapped the back window to get the driver's attention. As it rolled down, she said, "Excuse me, you seem to be lost. Do you know where you're going?"

"Um, yes. I think so. Don't worry," he responded.

Claudia didn't give up. "Don't worry? That's not working for me. Do you or do you not know where you are going?"

The driver didn't respond but continued to fumble with papers and ignore us. Clearly, he was lost.

"What time is it?" I asked.

One of my bridesmaids responded, "It's 11:02."

I was two minutes late to my wedding. I was late,

and my driver was lost. The night before, the priest had specifically said, "I start all my weddings on time. Don't be late." We were late!

I quickly assessed the situation. I looked outside again. I knew this was not the route to the church. Chris and I had driven the route, and I didn't remember any of these streets. What was I supposed to do? I closed my eyes and wished this wasn't happening. I had finally found the man of my dreams, it was our wedding day, and the limo driver was lost. It seemed impossible.

Claudia got off her phone. "I just tried calling everyone. They're all at the church and they must have turned off their phones. No one is picking up."

By then, we were ten minutes late. I started shaking. My heart screamed for Certainty. "Where are you? Where are you? How could you bring me this far in my journey only to get me lost on the way to the altar? This is not funny."

Certainty quickly calmed me down. "Have I ever failed you? Every time things get scary, you crack the door open to Doubt. You need to trust me. I'm here. First of all, you need to remember that I'm always here for you. Don't let your fears and doubts push me away, especially not today." I started to breathe more easily.

Certainty continued. "Good. Calm down. Now, this is a situation in which you do need to take action."

I took a few more deep breaths to calm down. Certainty said, "Now, pull yourself together." I looked around at the nervous faces, and then I yelled to the driver, "Please pull over!"

He was startled, but he continued to drive. I yelled again, "Pull over, right now! Right there into that fire station. We need to ask for directions."

The driver pulled our white limo into the fire station. One of my bridesmaids jumped out of the limo and ran toward the firehouse, nearly tripping over her bright-pink taffeta dress. About five firefighters were in the station, and they were clearly amused by the scene. From the window, I could see my friend explaining our situation to the firefighters. One of the men followed her back to the limo, tapped on the driver's window, and gave him detailed directions. All of the firefighters came over to us, waving and calling out hearty congratulations.

Dear Lord, please accept my prayer of thanks to this fire station, and please protect them always. Thank You, thank You, thank You. Amen.

We finally arrived at the church forty-five minutes late.

Dear Lord, thank You for bringing us here. Oh, and please forgive me my horrible thoughts about the physical harm I wanted to inflict on this driver. I am sorry—but seriously, what kind of limo driver gets lost between a hotel and church that are only five miles apart? But wait, I'm going backwards here. It's my wedding day, I'm here, and that's all that matters. My heart is full of joy.

Please forgive me, and thank You.

I could only imagine what was going through my groom's mind as he stood on the altar, waiting for me. The moment we arrived, the wedding party made its way into the church, and Dad and I waited our turn alone. He sneaked one quick kiss underneath my veil. "I love you." A broad victorious smile spread across his face, and he said, "The only thing I asked God for today was to let me walk you down the aisle, and He has."

I was confused. "Baba, of course you would walk me down the aisle. Why would you say something like that?"

His eyes looked tired. He didn't look well, but he continued to smile and said, "I love you, habibi."

Mendelssohn's Wedding March began. My heart began to race, my palms got sweaty, and my emotions were high. I'd heard this tune a hundred times as a guest or bridesmaid. I'd stood as a bridesmaid for at least twenty friends and relatives. Each time I heard the Wedding March, I prayed I'd hear it played for me someday. It was my day. They were playing it for me.

Dad wrapped his arm around mine as I fought back tears. We began our walk. Each step we took was down the aisle of a most picturesque Catholic Cathedral, adorned with stained glass and chandeliers and decorated with flowers and ribbons. At the end of the aisle, waiting for me, was my groom. The hour we stood in the church, side by side, taking our vows, was the most awe-inspiring hour of my life.

Dear Lord and our Blessed Virgin Mary, thank you for this miracle. Thank you for answering my prayer and showering me with this extraordinary miracle in my life.

After the final blessing had been bestowed, Chris and I shared our first kiss on the altar as husband and wife. We were married.

Later on, I whispered to Chris, "I'm sorry we were late. It must have been agonizing for you."

"I was a little concerned after I got your text that you had left and then the limo never showed up. But as I stood there on the altar, I knew the Lord would bring you here safely," he reassured me gently.

"What about everyone else?" I asked.

"Oh, that's a different story altogether. My siblings took bets on whether you had stood me up at the altar," he confessed.

"Seriously? They actually took bets in the church at our wedding?"

I was horrified. I called out for Certainty to help me work through this. "Please, help me understand. What is this supposed to teach me? Why would anyone take bets at their own brother's wedding?" Certainty laughed. "Welcome to the world of in-laws."

We have an old saying in my family. Expect at least one major disaster at your wedding and you won't be surprised. It was turning out to be true. At Claudia's wedding, her six hundred balloons were delivered to the wrong Church and then released. For Tina's wedding, her dress was a disaster. She allowed one of her friends to design it, and by the time she realized what an awful job he did, it was too late to order a new one. At Christian's wedding, the best man forgot the rings, resulting in a crazy, last-minute frenzy to get them. I assumed that a lost driver delivering me to the church forty-five minutes late was our disaster. I was wrong. More excitement awaited us at the reception.

The wedding planner was looking anxious as the bridal party arrived at the banquet hall. The cocktail hour was already in full swing, but our picturesque wedding day had turned into a blistering-hot June afternoon that was ruining most of the food artistically displayed outside on the veranda. Yes, everyone had warned me not to have the cocktail hour set up outside, but in my defense, the view was stunning, and I had made the decision back in February.

I was disappointed to see the ice sculpture melting beyond recognition. The stunning appetizers we had so painstakingly picked out were not palatable in the heat. Our guests had forsaken them and were desperately seeking the comfort of the indoor air-conditioning. Well, there was nothing I could do. There was no point in dwelling on a poor planning decision. We had the staff rescue what they could of the food outside and set up a new cocktail hour in another reception room.

Chris and I consciously invited Certainty to join us on our wedding day. This meant that, no matter what happened, we would experience our day with pure joy. We were determined to have fun.

Challenges continued to test our commitment to Certainty. Our photographer was missing half the time. We simply couldn't find him to take any formal family pictures. The live band ignored my playlist—the playlist I had spent four hours putting together and had my heart set on—and they performed their own songs. Whenever I requested a song, they smiled and ignored me. I was tempted to get upset, but then I'd remember our best friend and simply let it go.

Each time I successfully deflected my desire to react, I was tested again. We had set up a kids playroom with games and videos for entertainment and staffed with nannies. I thought the parents would love the plan and the kids would have more fun. Early into the reception, the wedding planner apprehensively informed me that all the children had escaped from the playroom and their parents were frantically looking for them. After the great kid escape, one of my new sister-in-laws threatened to leave the reception immediately. We were forced to improvise again and have a kid-friendly reception. The three nannies we had paid to watch the kids decided their job was done and headed straight to the bar. I never did figure out where they were when the kids escaped.

These challenges tested me sorely. I felt I had no authority at my own wedding. Again, I remembered the promise we had made to Certainty and let go.

Once that drama had been resolved, I noticed that the wedding planner was instructing the staff to rearrange tables. We'd had a teen table set up, and none of the teens sat there. Instead, they dragged chairs from nearby tables to sit with their parents. Other guests soon found their chairs were missing. No problem. We were becoming quite skilled at improvising.

Nothing bothered me very much because I was having the happiest day of my life. In fact, all of the little mishaps were amusing. They added a bit of color to our day. Inviting Certainty to the wedding meant extraordinary joy, no matter what happened.

Chris and I stole a few private moments together and all we could do was laugh. "I hate to admit this," I confided, "but I am avoiding the wedding planner. Every time I see her, she has a surprise waiting for us."

"It's all good." He smiled at me. It was one of Chris's favorite phrases. It always brought a smile to my face. I was deliriously happy.

"Everyone I know told us to avoid a big wedding and save our budget for the house," I said. "Boy, we should have listened! Since we didn't, let's get out there and enjoy the food." And so, we did. Chris and I are probably the only bride and groom in history who actually ate at their own wedding.

We had great fun despite all the dramas. We enjoyed the traditional wedding customs: the flamboyant introduction of the wedding party entering the reception, our first dance, the best man's toast, the garter-belt throw, the wedding cake on the face, and lots of dancing, definitely lots of dancing. In fact, the kids on the dance floor became the new hit of the reception, and may have had more fun than anybody else. My face ached from smiling so much.

When the bandleader announced it was time for the father of the bride to dance with his daughter, my dad was nowhere to be found. In fact, I realized I hadn't seen him since we left the church.

"Where is Baba? Where is Baba?" I went around asking my sisters. They looked at me nervously. I'd been so consumed with the reception dramas that

I had failed to notice the obvious. My own family was not having fun. In fact, they had been acting weird the whole time. I got an awful feeling in the pit of my stomach.

The bandleader stalled for an unusually long time. Everyone patiently waited for the father of the bride to appear. Then, from a side door, I saw Dad being led towards me by one of my cousins. My cousin was a medical resident. I realized he'd also been missing from the reception.

Dad took my hand, smiled, and led me in the father-daughter dance. As I held on to him, I knew something was wrong. Something was very wrong. As I danced with Dad, one tear fell down my face. I didn't know what was happening, but I said a silent prayer, thanking God for that moment. That moment changed everything. The drama and surprises of the reception evaporated instantly. I simply held onto my daddy and filled my heart with gratitude. After our dance, he kissed me and said he was going to relax in the bridal suite. I wouldn't allow my mind to invite a single negative thought. I hugged him tight and was grateful for our dance.

Following the formal reception, we held an after-party. All of our guests came back to the house. A DJ was waiting, and lots more food and drinks and fun. Chris and I danced until the early hours of the following morning.

Dad did not make it to the after-party. My family told me he was tired and wanted to stay back at the hotel to rest. I believed them. I'd had the most beautiful day in the world, and we'd had lots of fun. The day had exceeded any dream I ever imagined. Even the dramas didn't bother me, and I was able to laugh about them. The only thing that really worried me was that Dad was missing for most of the day.

Chapter 20

Set Sail...

We spent eight months planning the wedding. I meticulously project-managed every detail of the event. Hundreds of hours were spent researching, visiting vendors, developing power point presentations, preparing detailed spreadsheets, and budgeting. In the end, the event was over in the blink of an eye.

On the other hand, we booked our honeymoon in just a few hours. I told Chris I had only one criterion. I would go anywhere, but I did not want to get on a plane. I had spent the previous two years traveling the globe for my sales job. Airports were not fun for me; they were work. So, our challenge was to plan a great honeymoon without any flying. We booked a ten-day cruise from New York down to the

Caribbean. Not much planning was required, but in the end, they were the happiest ten days of my life.

Our honeymoon officially began in our suite on the stern of the ship as we popped open a bottle of champagne and said a toast to our new life. We made our way to the top deck and waved goodbye to New York as we set sail. Life was wonderful.

I was dancing with happiness until I realized that I was very nauseous. I'd never been on a cruise before. When I thought about it, I realized that it had been several years since the last time I had been on a boat. It was in Key West, a catamaran, and I had spent the entire time in the lower galley, sick to my stomach. I wondered how I could possibly have forgotten about that when we booked our honeymoon. It was official: I had severe seasickness.

I was scared that my entire honeymoon would be ruined. I had never felt so sick. Chris immediately bought me Dramamine. I felt so bad that I took twice the recommended dosage. It was not a good idea. I passed out for ten hours. After I regained consciousness, I said a few prayers. My prayers must have been heard, because, almost magically, I found my sea legs. I didn't get sick again, and I didn't need any more Dramamine.

Chris teased me about it. "You showed up late to the wedding, so it was only fitting that you would show up late to the honeymoon, too."

Chris and I are water people. There is nothing more magical than being out on the water, listening to the waves, watching the sun rise and set on the water, and enjoying the glory of one of God's greatest creations, His vast ocean. It's spectacular beyond words. This was the magic of our honeymoon.

We loved meeting the other newlyweds on board, as well as those celebrating milestone anniversaries. We met one couple who were celebrating sixty years together. Because our honeymoon overlapped both of our birthdays, every night was a celebration with the cruise staff singing "Happy Honeymoon" or "Happy Birthday." We were surrounded by joy. Everyone was in love, having fun, and laughing.

We also enjoyed eating our way through the buffet line, which is such a cliché, but very true. By our third day, I noticed that Chris mysteriously disappeared around three every afternoon. I quickly learned that three in the afternoon was Ben & Jerry's sundae hour on the forward deck. Chris hadn't wanted me to know about his ice cream addiction, little realizing how happy I was to share the addiction.

I'm still amazed that I had spent the eight months prior to our wedding going to the gym and doing yoga six days a week. Now, I was eating my way through the honeymoon. I had grown up with food as an expression of pure love. Holiday meals and family dinners were the greatest joy in life. We were simply full of love and joy.

Our honeymoon was perfect. On the last day, I felt overwhelmed with sadness as we packed our bags and headed towards the disembarkation area.

Chris could read my face. "Don't be sad. We have lots and lots of fun vacations ahead of us."

"I'd like you to promise me something," I began. "For our one-year anniversary, promise me we'll come back to the islands for a long weekend. Grand Turk was my favorite."

"That's a promise." He smiled at me.

As we enjoyed the last few moments in the disembarkation area, I decided to call Mom and Dad. I hadn't talked to anyone in my family since the wedding. Mom picked up on the first ring.

"Hi Momma," I began, excited. I joyously started sharing fun highlights and adventures from our honeymoon. She listened quietly without interrupting. As soon as I realized we were having a one-way conversation, which *never* happens with my mother, I stopped.

"Momma, what's wrong?" I asked.

"Nothing, habibi. Nothing. I'm glad you had such a wonderful honeymoon." Her voice told me this was not true.

"Momma, please. Just tell me. You are starting to scare me." Chris stopped what he was doing and focused his attention on my call.

"Jackie is your honeymoon over?" she asked.

It was a very odd question. "It is, now. Tell me what's going on."

"Jackie, your father had a stroke on your wedding day. We all agreed none of us would tell you until after your honeymoon."

"Momma, please, that can't be true. He danced with me." I was pleading.

"It happened afterwards."

"How is he now?" I desperately asked.

"Oh, Jackie, I don't know how to say this..." She paused for a long time. "He has brain cancer.

The tumor is in a bad location. He needs surgery, but his chances of surviving the surgery are less than eight percent. Without the surgery, he'll have only another month. He wants the surgery. We've been waiting for you to come home, to give you a chance to see him before..." Her words trailed off.

My honeymoon officially ended with my new husband holding me as I broke into uncontrollable sobbing.

Chapter 21

What is a Miracle?

On my wedding day, the first words I wrote in my journal were, 'What Is a Miracle?' Pondering the unknown journey of marriage and the path ahead of us, I saw it as a seed, a beginning. All day, I prayed to see the miracle in the seed, and not only after the first petals had bloomed.

God in his infinite wisdom continued to teach me. He gave me the miracle of a father walking his daughter down the aisle and sharing one last dance on her wedding day. He taught me that I am surrounded by miracles. A father simply dancing with his daughter is one of the greatest miracles my heart treasures.

Heartache and challenge followed the happiest days of my life. The day following our honeymoon, I flew to Florida to see Dad. My new husband endured endless jokes from his sisters about his new bride ditching him so soon. Bets were placed on whether I was planning to come back. My heart ached as jokes were being made at our expense. Throughout all, my husband was my bedrock of unconditional love and support.

Upon landing at the airport, I drove my rental car straight to the hospital. With a heavy heart, I saw Dad in ICU, holding onto his life. The last time I had seen him we were dancing. My family and the doctors had been keeping him comfortable for two weeks while waiting for me to return. No one said it, but they were waiting for me to say goodbye.

I called upon Certainty to give me strength in this difficult hour. "My dear friend, please help me. Please help me find the courage." I sat with Dad for hours and prayed at his bedside. I felt Certainty in my heart, whispering to me, "It's not his time, yet." At first, the whisper was faint. When I didn't listen, Certainty spoke in a louder voice. "It's not his time." These words kept ringing louder and louder.

Dad's situation seemed impossible. The neurosurgeon had explained that this was an extraordinarily difficult surgery and that Dad's chances of survival were very slim. If he did survive, he might still suffer brain damage and paralyzing effects from the stroke. The doctors had actually advised him to go home and enjoy his last month. Even Dad's own medical team had no Hope.

Nonetheless, Certainty spoke more and more loudly, repeating the same words to me. Finally, I was able to listen and stop weeping. I stopped praying for a dad who was already gone and instead thanked the

Lord for another chance. I kissed Dad's forehead and told him confidently, "I will see you when you wake up from surgery."

I did see him. Against amazing odds, Dad survived his surgery. It was nothing short of remarkable. His cancerous tumor was successfully removed, and his own neurosurgeon seemed shocked that Dad was still alive.

I spent a lot of time with him during recovery. He slipped in and out of consciousness. Sometimes, he spoke, but I'm not sure he knew what he was saying.

One morning when we were alone, Dad looked deep into my eyes and said, "They let me come back."

I was puzzled. "Who did, Baba?"

I'm not sure he was talking to me or knew I was there, but he continued. "They said I could come back because I refused to go the hospital."

"Baba, what are you talking about? You're in the hospital, now. What are you trying to say?" I pleaded.

"I wouldn't let them take me...I wouldn't let them ruin the wedding," he mumbled deliriously.

"Baba, please, what are you talking about?" I tried again. It was no use. He lost consciousness.

Had I imagined it? I repeated his words repeatedly in my head and couldn't make sense of what he was trying to tell me.

Later that evening, while I was having dinner with Mom and my siblings, I asked all of them, "What exactly happened with Baba on the day of my wedding?"

Claudia told me the whole story.

"Jackie, as soon as we awoke that morning, we all knew something was very wrong. Daddy hadn't slept all night. He was completely numb on his entire right side. He couldn't move his right arm and couldn't see out of his right eye. He was unresponsive and confused. He was dizzy and couldn't walk. He said he was having a severe headache. I knew he was having a stroke. I just knew. I begged him to let me take him to the hospital. I begged him to call an ambulance. I told him if he didn't go to hospital right away, a stroke could kill him. I begged him, but he refused. He kept saying,'I don't care if I die. I don't care if I die. I'm not going to ruin her wedding. I am going to walk my daughter down the aisle.'

During the reception, he got worse. We kept him comfortable in the bridal suite and again begged him to go to the hospital. He continued to refuse. He just kept saying, 'I don't care if I die. I won't ruin her wedding day.' He also told us if anyone said anything to you, he would never forgive us or speak to us again.

"He could barely walk and couldn't move his right side at all. None of us could figure out how he got up to dance with you. Later on, during your after-party, we finally took him to the hospital. We learned he had had a stroke. A few days later, they found the cancer."

What is a miracle? *It is the power of Love.*

Chapter 22

My Announcement

When does life begin? The question gets people's attention and makes them immediately draw up battle lines. If a writer agrees with my views, I will respect her and continue reading. If she disagrees, I must disregard everything. However, this is not a set up to a heated debate. I've simply been thinking about the question a lot lately.

When does life end? Most people don't argue about that one. They just presume it's at the moment we call death. Of course, the Church promises us that eternal life exists in the heavenly kingdom.

As I wrote in my journal, I was not surrounded by fresh-cut flowers. It was raining outside and gloomy. My thoughts were a bit on the heavy side. I was seated at Dad's bedside. I could hear him breathing through his oxygen mask. He had just gotten another dose of morphine and was sound asleep.

Six months before, Dad had miraculously survived his surgery and was given another chance at life. We cherished having him back in full health for about four months, which was a pure gift from heaven. Then, the cancerous brain tumor returned and quickly spread to his lungs. This time it was inoperable. He was assigned a hospice nurse who came to the house every day. She told us he had only a few weeks at the most, and that had been two months ago.

Christmas was ten days away. Mom had not put up a tree. We asked her to, but she just couldn't do it. The house showed no signs of the upcoming holiday. Instead, hospice had set up Dad's hospital bed in the living room where there was more space. Carefully marked and organized in bundles, medical supplies and medications filled the corners of the dining room. I tried and tried, but I could not find any Christmas spirit there.

My flight home to New York was a few hours away. I had flown back and forth several times over the last two months, each time without knowing if it would be our last time together. Now, I patiently waited for Dad to wake up. I had something to tell him before I left.

My thoughts took me back in time to my childhood. Memories of playing with Dad in the backyard, his famous barbeques, and his spaghetti night dinners popped into my head. My fondest memories were of him, singing. He was a most talented musician and had loved to entertain us for hours. He always had a happy disposition. He kept smiling even on cloudy days, and he could find the good in any situation.

Dad stirred and started to wake up. Slowly, he opened his eyes. He let me know he could see me by forming a small smile. I held his hand and quickly prepared myself to share my news. I didn't know how long he would be awake.

"Baba. Baba, I have something I want to tell you. We're having a baby. You're going to have another grandchild," I said, struggling to keep back my tears.

He held my hand tightly, smiled, and said, "I love you, habibi. Congratulations."

I ached. I was three months pregnant with my first child and holding the hand of my father, who had been bravely fighting death for two months. One life was growing inside me, while the one who gave me life was slowly leaving. I could not make sense of it.

I prayed for Certainty to give me courage. Certainty came to me and said, "It is now time for you to say goodbye. Take comfort in the promise of eternal life."

I kissed Dad one last time. A single tear rolled down his face as he said, "I love you."

Those were the last words my daddy ever spoke to me.

Chapter 23

Our First Christmas

Midnight Mass on Christmas Eve was inspiring. The choir sang the holiday hymns joyously, a group of children performed the nativity scene, and the congregation radiated joy. On this day, the Savior was born, and my heart was full of emotion.

As the Eucharist was being prepared, I stood in the pew next to my husband, one hand holding his and the other on my belly to connect to our child. I remembered the Church of Nativity and the Star of Bethlehem. I stood there, feeling the holy place where the Lord chose to be born. Only a few blocks away from that church, in a small house, my Dad also had been born. Now, he was ready to go home. I prayed to the Lord...

Our Heavenly Father, thank you for the miracle of your Son and the joy of this day. One of your children is ready to come home. He's suffered enough. I beg you to welcome him home to your eternal kingdom and give him peace in his eternal life. In the name of your Son and in the miracle and glory of this day, please shower him with peace and eternal life in your heavenly kingdom.

After Mass, the priest spent a few extra moments with me, praying for Dad. He gave me strength, courage, and the gift of peace in my heart.

When I had called Mom earlier that night, she confirmed that Dad was still unconscious. He'd not woken up in three days. Two and half months before, the doctors had told us he had only a few weeks at most, but Dad was a fighter. He was still with us. My sisters and brother were down in Florida to spend the holiday with Mom. Chris and I were scheduled to fly down the day after Christmas. I would get to see Dad again in less than two days.

I awoke on Christmas morning, remembering a vivid dream. I had been having a lot of lucid dreams since I'd been pregnant, but this one was different. I dreamed of a choir of angels singing, preparing for a guest.

The ringing of the phone startled me out of bed. I looked over at the clock. It was 9:05 a.m. I never slept so late, but we hadn't gotten home from Mass until the early hours of the morning. I had found I needed a lot more sleep because of the pregnancy. The phone rang at least five or six times before I could get to it.

I figured it was my family, calling to wish us a Merry Christmas.

"Hello," I said in my groggy morning voice.

"He's gone." Claudia's voice was full of tears. "Jackie, he's gone. It was early this morning. I was holding his hand when he left."

My heart was devastated. I was in agony. I wouldn't get to see him the next day as I had planned. I would never see him again. My husband wrapped his arms around me and held me as I wept for my daddy.

Two hours later, we attended the family Christmas Mass at church. I could easily have stayed home. I'm sure no one would have judged me for such a decision on that day, but I needed to go. I wiped away all my tears and entered the church with a heart full of gratitude. I thanked the Lord for bringing my father home while he slept and ending his earthly suffering. I also prayed that He would bless us with comfort and ease our suffering.

After Mass, the priest who had prayed with me the night before asked about Dad. "He went home this morning," I told him. "He choose to go home to celebrate Christmas with the Lord." Tears rolled down my face as my effort to control my emotions gave way.

The priest held my hand and prayed. He told me, "I prayed for him last night, and then I dreamed of a choir of angels singing."

"So did I, Father. So did I."

Each of us has a choice. We can always choose how we react to situations and how we feel. I cried a lot that day, but I choose to cry tears of joy. There are no tears of sadness on Christmas.

I chose to remember the day with joy in my heart. I chose to continue honoring this day as the day my Savior was born, and now it was also the day my Dad chose to begin his eternal life. He chose to spend the holiday with the Lord, and the choirs of angels were ready to welcome him.

I chose then and I choose now to remember that day as a Christmas Miracle.

Chapter 24

Happy Anniversary

My labor began at two a.m. on a Thursday morning. I was four days past my due date and looking forward to finally having the baby. For the first three hours, I had mild contractions that came about twenty minutes apart. During those early morning hours, I lay in bed dreaming about our new life and how everything was about to change. I also felt a little sad. The baby and I had a special relationship, our own bond. She had been all mine and I didn't have to share her. That was about to change.

The sun peeked through the blinds. Chris woke up. In a muzzy voice, he asked, "Is today the day?" I quickly debated sneaking in one more jab about how easy his job was compared to what I was about to face. I decided not to ruin the moment.

I'd been listening to meditation CDs designed to calm me during labor and started repeating happy mantras. I wanted to maintain a happy and blissful state during the labor to ensure that the baby would be happy and blissful.

"Yes, I think today is the day. I've been in labor for hours." I calculated that we'd have the baby by late that afternoon or perhaps early evening.

Chris and I had gone to all the childbirth classes. The coach continually emphasized that there was no such thing as an "average" delivery. Each woman was unique. I didn't really care what average was. I believed in the power of positive thinking and was determined to have a wonderful and quick delivery.

"Okay, when do we call the doctor? Should we get ready to go to the hospital?" Apparently, Chris was just as impatient as I was.

"I don't think we're ready, yet. Doctor said I needed to wait until the contractions were five to six minutes apart before heading to the hospital. Right now, they're sporadic—twenty to thirty minutes apart."

Chris jumped into the shower to get ready for work, and I stayed in bed to enjoy that wonderful, happy morning. My baby will be born today, I said to myself. I wanted to enjoy this special day as much as possible. So far, the contractions had been only mildly uncomfortable. I told myself I could handle labor, that it was going to be a piece of cake. I was determined to have a natural labor, but I was keeping the option of an epidural open. I *might* consider it if labor became too difficult. However, I was determined to be strong and do this on my own. That's what was best for the baby.

Within hours, the contractions got a lot worse. By mid-afternoon, each contraction felt like a machete thrust on my lower back, so that I lost my breath. It was not fun, anymore.

I calmed myself a bit by thinking that I must be getting closer to having the baby. That was it. It must be time. Except for one thing: the contractions were completely sporadic, two minutes apart, then twenty, then an hour. This was not how it was supposed to go. The calm, serene, happy labor I planned was turning into a panic attack. The contractions were pure torture.

I called Chris. "Honey, something is wrong. This pain, it's not like the videos we saw in class. It's bad, I mean really, really bad."

Chris tried to calm me down, "Do you think you're ready to go to the hospital?"

"Yes, let's go. I want an epidural."

"What do you mean you want an epidural? I thought you wanted a natural labor. Isn't that better for the baby?"

"Seriously, seriously! You're going to argue with me on this? You have no idea how bad this is!"

I told myself to calm down. I told myself not to yell at my husband. I told myself to remember happy labor for the baby. Happy labor. Besides, everyone gets an epidural. You're not a bad mother if you get one. Just them, I had another contraction. It lasted thirty-four seconds. I couldn't breathe. It was unbearable. But my dilemma was solved: I was definitely getting the epidural.

"Yes, honey. I'm ready to go to the hospital."

That Thursday afternoon was our first trip to the hospital. After a month of research and visiting the labor delivery units of three different hospitals, Chris and I chose a hospital that was a forty-minute drive from our house. It was far, but I was convinced that it was the best place to have the baby. I strolled in happily and told the guard, "I'm here to have a baby." He offered us a big smile and his congratulations then pointed towards the elevators leading to the labor unit.

The waiting room was empty, and within ten minutes, I was being pre-examined by the nurse on duty.

"You're not ready, yet. I can't admit you. Go back home and come back when the contractions are five minutes apart."

"Nurse, you don't understand. The contractions are really, really bad. It's like a bulldozer or a machete in my back. I can't take it."

"I'm sorry. It's sounds like you're having back labor. Try soaking in the tub or doing light exercises like squatting or lunging."

"Are you kidding me? That's your advice? I don't want to exercise. I want an epidural!"

I was sent home.

The contractions got worse and worse. I was in pure agony. Each contraction lasted twenty-five to forty seconds, and I stopped breathing during each one. The contractions literally knocked the wind out of me. I had never experienced such excruciating pain in my life.

Chris attempted to coach me. "Honey, try those breathing exercises we learned in class. That might help."

"Nothing is helping!"

It was not going as planned. I wanted a happy and calm labor. This agony exceeded my ability to imagine it. How had women been having babies since the beginning of time if they had to go through this? It was so awful. I just didn't understand.

The next twenty-four hours were torture. By then, it was Friday morning. I called my doctor, wanting reassurance and comfort that what I was experiencing was normal. "You're definitely in back labor. It's beyond awful. Do you want to come in for a c-section?" she asked.

"No. I can't. I need to have this baby naturally—oh, I mean naturally with an epidural." I needed to add that caveat.

"Okay. If you're determined to have this baby naturally, then come in when the contractions are five minutes apart. As long as you're in advanced labor, we can administer the epidural."

At this point, I offered a little white lie. "Okay. We're coming in. They're five minutes apart."

Friday afternoon was our second trip to the hospital.

That time, a young female intern examined me. She was very petite and bubbly. Normally, I would have instantly liked her, but right then I couldn't handle the bubbly energy.

"You're still not ready. We need to send you home again."

"What! Are you kidding me? I've been in back labor for over thirty hours! Something is not right. I need to have this baby, now."

"I'm sorry, but you're just not ready. Try soaking in the tub or light exercises like lunging or squatting."

I had gotten the same speech the day before. Were they all trained to give the same canned speech? It was obvious to me that none of these women had ever been in labor. They wouldn't give out such smug, textbook advice if they knew what back labor really was.

For the second time, I was sent home to somehow endure my own private torture. It seemed impossible that I had been in labor for over thirty hours and everyone was telling me I wasn't ready.

On the drive back home from the hospital, I could hear Chris on the phone with someone from the family, "No, not yet. Another false alarm. We're on our way back home."

Another false alarm? That was how he saw this?

"Another false alarm! Are you kidding me? I'm in labor, and you casually dismiss what's going on as another false alarm!"

"Honey, we live forty minutes from the hospital. We can't keep driving back and forth. All the doctors keep saying the same thing: We have to wait until the contractions are five minutes apart."

"Honey, pull into Sports Authority. I want to buy a bat and pound it into your back and then see how you feel. Tell me then that it's a another false alarm!"

It was not the happy labor I planned. Every contraction weakened me more, and I saw I had become one of those women who take it out on her husband. I vowed I would not become one of those women.

The movies and TV shows are all lies, filmed by directors who've never had kids. On TV, everybody's water breaks, they're happy, their make-up is perfect, and one commercial break later, there's a baby. That's how I was expecting this to be. I was even planning to do my make-up. I wanted to be pretty for the baby. I did not think this was a crazy notion, not at all.

I had never heard of back labor. I had never heard of any woman being in labor for so long! Another big fat lie is, "You'll forget once the baby is born." Oh, I didn't think so! Yes, I would love my baby more than anything on the planet, but I don't think it's humanly possible to forget torture! Yes, torture. How does one magically forget being tortured?

I came to the conclusion that our mothers tell us we'll forget because, after thirty or forty years, they've simply forgotten a lot of things, and giving birth to their kids is just one more thing on that list. No, I was not going to forget this. In fact, my daughter would hear the story often and for the rest of her life.

Friday night leading into Saturday morning was awful. I resorted to crying. Every contraction sent me into tears. There were seven billion people on the planet, and I just could not comprehend how seven billion mothers had endured this. How is it our species didn't die out? How could a woman voluntarily have relations again after enduring this? Labor was sheer torture. There was nothing natural about it. How could anyone call it natural labor?

I kept flashing back to one of my favorite books during middle school, Pearl Buck's *The Good Earth.* In a vivid and poignant scene, the wife O-Lan, was working in the rice fields, went into labor, had the baby all by herself, and then went back to work in the fields the same day. I hadn't thought about that book in twenty years. I thought about all the women who've brought a child into this world. I'd never appreciated the sacrifice moms make. It's a special, secret club. No matter how many times you read about this club, watch it on TV and movies, and try to imagine it, it is impossible to understand if you're not a mother. No, it wasn't easy, but I continually reminded myself that this was my initiation into the club. It was also a huge lesson in appreciation for mothers everywhere.

On Saturday morning, I called my doctor in tears. I told her the agony was unbearable, and I was afraid if I came back to the hospital and was sent home again, I might physically attack the examining nurse.

She told me to come in and I would be put on therapeutic bed rest. She promised I wouldn't be sent home again.

Therapeutic bed rest? What was that? Why was I only learning of it, then? Why hadn't anyone told me about this magical thing called therapeutic bed rest two days before? I had no idea what it was, but it sounded good to me.

On Saturday afternoon, Chris and I made our third trip back to the hospital. The guard who was there on Thursday was back on duty. He was surprised when he saw me. "What happened? I thought you had your baby days ago?"

I made the only reply I could think of, "Labor isn't going as planned."

"Today is the day. I feel it," he announced with a radiant smile.

For the first time in two days, I returned a smile and reminded myself I was having a baby. This was the day, just like the guard said. I also reminded myself I was on my way to this wonderful thing called therapeutic bed rest. I was just one quick elevator ride away from it.

We checked in as soon as we got upstairs, and I expected to be admitted within five minutes. I noticed things were moving slowly, maybe because it was a Saturday.

Another contraction. I needed to get admitted.

"Um, excuse me, but I've been here for over fifteen minutes. My doctor is waiting for me."

"Yes, your doctor is doing rounds. You need to wait for an available nurse, and we don't have any right now. You just need to wait."

I waited for an hour and a half, having contractions every five to seven minutes in front of dozens of observers in the waiting room. My serenity had completely vanished. I yelled and threatened the staff, and yes, I admit was a bit disagreeable.

Finally, at three p.m., I was admitted. I asked the nurse how quickly I could get an epidural. She made a smug little joke. "Your birth plan indicates you want a natural birth."

It took every ounce of my self-control not to hit her. I thought that, under the circumstances, God probably would forgive me. But no, I couldn't hit her. Instead, I replied calmly, "It's not a good idea to joke around with a woman who has been in back labor for two and half days."

She clearly heard the warning in my voice. "I understand. I'll page the anesthesiologist."

One hour later, this young, hip, Irish doctor sporting funny sneakers walked into my room. He introduced himself as the anesthesiologist. I'd never been more relieved to meet anyone in my life. If my childhood idol Madonna had walked in at that same moment and offered me my own private concert, I would have quite happily turned her down for my epidural.

By then, I was crying full out. The pain was unbearable, and I was delirious. After the epidural was in place, I looked at the young doctor, who barely looked old enough to practice medicine and affectionately announced, "Doctor, I love you."

"Yeah, I get that a lot in my job," he casually acknowledged.

After two and half days of labor, I finally had gotten my epidural.

Hours went by, and labor wasn't progressing. I got a round of Pictocin, again something I had clearly vowed not to do on my birth plan. By then, my birth plan had become something of a joke. I had spent months planning and researching every aspect of labor. I typed up a beautiful, six-page birth plan, complete with research citations, and had it printed on thick-stock pink paper. I created about two dozen "birth plan gift bags" for the labor and delivery and maternity ward staffs. Each shiny silver gift bag was adorned with pink ribbons and bows. Inside were the birth plan, chocolates, candy, and a popular CD as a thank you gift from the baby. I instructed Chris to hand out the bags to the nurses and doctors on staff.

Every time I met someone new on staff, I was introduced as "the birth plan lady" with the pink gift bags.

One nurse who came in to check my IV bag was humming as she did her job and had a calm and reassuring presence. I liked her. After she was finished, she looked at me with great sincerity and said, "Thank you for the gift bag. It was very lovely."

"Really? It seems like a joke, right now. Two nurses almost denied me my epidural because of that silly birth plan."

"Oh, honey, they were just kidding with you. The fact is, we were all very impressed. You did quite a bit of research to put that plan together. I've never seen anything like it."

That got me excited—validation! "Really? You like it? You're not just saying that?" I felt almost like a student who had passed a test.

"It was an excellent plan, but…things aren't exactly going as you planned."

"No. For years, I've practiced this totally organic lifestyle—no meds, no fast food, and lots of water and yoga. I envisioned a peaceful, calm, serene birth. I've been doing positive mantras and affirmations for months, but...back labor—once those contractions hit, everything went out the window and I became a screaming, threatening tyrant."

She chuckled. "Yes, I have to admit I was a bit surprised to realize the "birth plan gift bag lady" was the same woman who came in here crying and yelling at everyone."

"Was I really that bad?" I wondered.

"Oh please. You're in labor. Don't apologize to anyone."

"I also developed a Power Point presentation for my husband with instructions." I was so happy to get approval for my birth plan that I started looking for extra credit validation.

"Oh, I'm sure he loved that."

Was that sarcasm I heard? Okay. No extra credit on the presentation. "I feel foolish now, but I really wanted a perfect natural birth. Is there anything wrong with that?" I asked.

"Sweetie, there's no such thing as perfect. Each birth is unique and beautiful, as is each baby being born. Use this experience to prepare you for motherhood. Nothing will ever go as planned. You'll spend months planning things for your kids, and all those plans will fall apart in minutes. That's life. And forgive yourself. No one expects you to be perfect."

Good advice for a new mother-to-be.

The monitors started blinking and making lots of noise. A nurse hurried in to check and I could see panic register on her face. Immediately, Chris was rushed out of the room. A team of doctors and nurses stormed in. The baby's vitals were crashing. The baby was crashing. Pray, pray, pray, I told myself. What is going on? Pray.

O dear Mary, Mother of the Lord, please protect our baby. Please, please protect our baby. Please forgive me for breaking my vow to have a happy labor. Please protect our baby. Please protect our baby. Three Hail Mary's... Our Father who art in Heaven... Glory Be...

What other prayers did I know? I tried to think. Certainty, please, where are you? Please protect our baby.

One minute, two minutes, five minutes. It was the longest eternity of my life. My mind was lost in prayer. Finally, my doctor stabilized us. The monitors stopped blinking, and the doctors slowly filtered out of my room.

"What happened?" I cried.

"It looks like the baby didn't like the Pictocin."

I was exhausted. I never imagined labor could be like this. I reeled from the scare and spent the next few hours watching the monitor register each contraction, just waiting and waiting and waiting. No progress. Our baby clearly had a mind of her own. She was just not ready.

I hate to admit it, but I was bored and just wanted to talk. I looked over at Chris. I talked for about ten minutes before I realized he wasn't answering me. I nudged him, and he pulled a set of earphones out. "What are you doing?" I demanded.

He responded nervously, "Nothing."

"What do you mean nothing? What are you doing? Are those earphones?"

When he turned around completely, I could see that he had the portable DVD player in his lap and was watching *Pirates of the Caribbean*. Seriously, I was in labor, and he was watching a movie.

"Seriously? Seriously? What was the point of us taking all those stupid childbirth classes? You're supposed to be my coach, coach me through this."

"Honey, you got the epidural. I don't know what I'm supposed to do, now. There's nothing left to coach."

"So you decided to watch a movie?"

"Come on. You have to admit, it's a great movie."

That proved it. A mother going through labor and a father supporting his wife through labor are not in the same category and can never be compared. By then, though, I was just too tired to care or to argue. I turned around and continued to watch my contractions on the monitor. I loved the epidural. It was the greatest invention since the beginning of time.

More hours passed. No progress.

"Happy Anniversary, honey!" Chris leaned over and kissed me.

"What?" I was confused.

"Happy Anniversary! Honey, it just turned midnight. It's officially our one-year wedding anniversary."

Our one-year wedding anniversary. My mind couldn't comprehend it.

"Happy anniversary, honey."

At the end of our honeymoon, I had told Chris I wanted to spend our one-year wedding anniversary on an island, sipping a Margarita and running through the sand. I wanted a nice, long weekend getaway.

Now there we were, a year later. The baby had been due seven days before and I had been in back labor for three days. My labor was failing to progress, and the Pictocin did nothing but give us a good scare. The baby wasn't showing any intention of wanting to join us.

Chris could read my thoughts. "This is not the island vacation I promised you."

"No, but we're having a baby."

"Okay, I'll make a you a deal. I'll give you an IOU on the island vacation to be redeemed sometime in the next ten years, and in the meantime, I see a lot of Disney vacations in our future."

I started laughing, "Disney, it is."

Now that was something to look forward to—Disney with my family. It was another chance to make a dream come true.

After another hour, my vitals started crashing. My blood pressure plummeted. I was dizzy and losing consciousness. Later, I reviewed my medical records and saw that I was undergoing serious internal hemorrhaging due to the stress placed on my body from the long labor. The baby soon followed my lead, and her vitals crashed again. The doctors also feared she was taking in meconium.

The natural and intimate birth I meticulously planned for months was not an option. We were rushed in for an emergency c-section. I watched an army of doctors from NICU join us in my delivery. They were anxiously preparing to take our baby as soon as she was born.

I wouldn't get to hold her, bond with her, nurse her, or establish that instant connection that every single website claimed was so critical. We were being prepped for an emergency c-section.

I was facing the greatest fear of my life: the safe delivery of our daughter. I had just seconds to decide if I was going to face it with certainty or let doubt sneak in.

I'd been through so many challenges in my life, many of which I failed. I spent years fixing those failures and learning the true meaning of certainty. Now that I was going to be a mother, I needed to be strong. I told myself that my life would never again be my own. I was a mother, now, and I must bring our daughter into this world with certainty and love.

Chris was my rock. His presence continually reminded me I would not have to face this challenge alone. He held my trembling hand, pushed my hair away from my face, and also remained strong in the company of his own fear. He continually repeated those simple and magical words, "I love you."

As the baby was being delivered, I had flashbacks of every lesson I have learned in my life. Nothing has ever happened as planned. I guess that's the only promise we ever get in our lives: that nothing will ever go as planned.

Yes, a tiny part of me was still scared, but my prayers and the love of my soul mate gave me strength. I kept silently repeating my prayers and felt myself embraced with the warm blanket of certainty.

Dear Lord and the Blessed Virgin Mary, please protect our baby as she enters this world. I beg you with every ounce of my being, please protect our baby.

The voice of pure love, the tender voice of my friend, reminded me that He was there. "I'm here… I'm here for you, and I will protect the baby." I knew that voice so well: it was my dearest companion, Certainty. "Thank you," I whispered as silent tears rolled down my face.

"I will protect the baby all the days of her life," Certainty promised me. The baby was delivered. She had a loud and healthy cry. My doctor yelled, "It's a girl. It's a beautiful, healthy, baby girl!"

I summoned every ounce of strength I had. From behind a curtain, I spoke to our daughter for the first time, "It's Momma. It's Momma. I love you."

Tears poured down my face. Chris was trembling with relief. Our daughter was healthy, and she was crying. I was a momma. As soon as she heard my voice, she stopped crying. She knew me. She knew my voice. She knew our love. I knew she felt safe and happy.

The NICU team took her, did all the necessary exams, and determined she was not in any danger. After twenty minutes, Chris helped bundle her up and brought her over to me. I saw our daughter for the first time. Our eyes locked, and my soul trembled with pure love. “I love you, Josephine Mary. It’s Momma. It’s Momma.”

Our daughter made her way into this world with quite a bang. By the grace of the Lord and our prayers to the Blessed Virgin, we had a safe delivery.

By the way, I was wrong. The moment I saw her, I did forget the pain.

Chapter 25

The Pinecone

I keep a pinecone on the fireplace mantel. I love pinecones. About ten years ago, I learned what I call the "lesson of pinecones."

It was a crisp fall day, and I was hiking in the beautiful Hudson Valley Mountains in New York. It was one of my solitude hikes to connect to nature, clear my mind, and think. Halfway up a path, I came across a tour group. The guide was giving the group a history of the region. The path was too narrow for me to pass the group, so I waited patiently behind them.

The guide picked up a pinecone. "Does anyone know why this pinecone is one of nature's greatest miracles?"

A few people attempted a guess. The guide listened and then continued, "Those are all good guesses." He paused dramatically, building up suspense, "Pinecones give birth *to new life* in the presence of fire."

He waited like the perfect storyteller to make sure his audience was actively listening. By then, I was intrigued and made sure I heard every word.

He continued, "Yes, it's true. The pinecone *evolves* in fire. You see, most of us view fire as something destructive. A forest fire can quickly spread devastation on nature. However, fires actually are necessary for forest regeneration. The fire will consume the dead, decaying vegetation and clear the way for new growth. This pinecone," he held it up high for dramatic effect, "this pinecone will explode in a fire. Its seeds will spread across the forest and allow the forest to re-grow."

That day, I picked up a pinecone and really examined it for the first time in my life. I repeated to myself over and again, "The pinecone evolves and spreads new life in the presence of fire."

I had heard the story of the pinecone in the aftermath of the tragedies that nearly consumed and destroyed my life. At the time, I was still very angry and struggling. I suppose I felt that a forest fire had swept through my life, and I couldn't see past the devastation and damage. The pinecone reminded me that, if God gave nature this remarkable gift to heal itself after a fire, then He also must have a gift for all of us. It took me a few years to figure out what that gift was, but eventually I did. The pinecone in life *is prayer*. In the wake of fire and devastation, prayer has always been the answer that carried the seed to healing and growth.

As I roll the pinecone back and forth in my hands, I look back at the past year. Prayer does not mean that all of our challenges instantly disappear. There's an old saying that everything happens in threes. That certainly held true for me in the past year. The three challenges were Dad having a stroke on my wedding day, Dad leaving the world on Christmas morning, and the baby and I fighting for our lives during the first few hours of my one-year wedding anniversary. Those were a Big Three. Prayer didn't eliminate these challenges, but it did give me the opportunity to face them with courage and, of course, with Certainty.

A smile spreads across my face as I realize I have kept a pinecone nearby for over ten years now. It provides a life lesson that is both simple and profound. For me, the pinecone is a constant reminder of appreciation. I appreciate it as nature's miracle of growth in the wake of fire. It reminds me that fires cannot destroy us unless we let them. They clear out the dead and decaying elements in our life to make way for something new. I'm reminded of another familiar saying I have heard in church: "If things don't go your way, it just means that God has something better planned for you."

The baby has started crying. She's up from her nap early today, which means my reflections will have to wait until later. I put down my pinecone and hurried up to the nursery.

She's only a week old, and I'm still trying to figure out the rules of motherhood. Am I doing this right? What if I mess up? Does she know how much I love her? Will this euphoria I'm feeling from new motherhood crash from the extreme lack of sleep? Will she ever figure out her days and nights? Will I ever figure out how to adjust if she continues to stay up all night and sleep all day? Will I get the chance to take a shower today? When did a shower turn into a luxury? These are all fleeting thoughts. The fact is, I am high on life. There are simply no words in this world to describe my joy and love.

"Honey, Chris! You have to come up here. Come up," I yelled with giddy excitement. "Come up!"

Chris quickly rushed in.

"Her first smile! Look, look…she's smiling," I joyously announced.

"Um, I don't think she's smiling, I think she has gas. She's still too young to smile," he declared.

"Seriously," I began my warning tone, "don't ruin this moment for me. I'm declaring this her first smile."

"Okay, okay, put this down in your keepsake journal. It's her first smile," he relented. Then he quickly added, "But just in case, let's still burp her."

These are the treasured moments of my life, the moments my heart memorizes and keeps hidden in a secret place. The first time my daughter smiled back is one of my greatest treasures.

I often ask myself what I did to deserve such an amazing life. How many times have I fallen? How many times have I been broken and left to stare at the shattered pieces of my life? How many times have

I felt that a fire has destroyed and consumed my life? Were all those fires really a gift to clear the path for this amazing life I'm living right now?

I don't know all the answers, but I do remind myself that, even in the darkest moments, I was always able to find a small, flickering light. The light that leads to new beginnings, like the pinecone for the forest, is always prayer.

Chapter 26

Eternal Love

Today is my thirty-fourth birthday, and the first one I get to celebrate as a new momma. The baby is now ten days old. Her first present to me was sleeping four straight hours through the night. I actually woke up feeling mildly well rested and had a little bounce in my step. She was still sleeping as I slipped downstairs.

Chris placed an enormous bouquet of roses on the dining room table. It was waiting for me with a card. One dozen white roses, one dozen red roses, and one dozen yellow roses, artistically arranged with baby's breath. My birthday card read:

> "My dearest love…
>
> The white roses represent all of our new beginnings, the red represent our love, and the

yellow represent our joy and friendship. You are simply my everything…my new beginning, my soul mate, my love, my best friend. You mean more to me than these simple words can ever explain.

I love you, Happy Birthday."

Happy tears fell down my cheeks as I appreciated the beauty of his gift and my husband's romantic inspiration. For several days, I had been telling Chris that the only thing I wanted for my birthday was a couple of quiet hours alone to write in my journal and say my prayers. He was upstairs with the baby as I prepared to head to one of my favorite places—the beach.

I love the beach. I find few places more soothing than this wondrous creation. The rhythmic crashing of the waves against the shoreline, set against the backdrop of the vast, endless ocean always calms me. The only rival for my admiration in terms of beauty is the sun when she is rising or setting along the ocean's horizon. This is where my soul connects to God, where I can hear the voices of the angels and saints in heaven, and where I come to reflect. As I take in the splendor surrounding me, the overwhelming feeling that fills my heart is gratitude.

Dear Lord,

Thank You for another birthday to celebrate life. Thank You for all the gifts You've given me. Thank You for all the miracles. Thank You for my soul mate. Thank You for our daughter. Thank You for Your eternal love.

Simply... thank You for everything.

As I'm writing, I hear that familiar voice of love. "May I join you?" Certainty asks.

My heart is bursting with happiness. "Always. You are my best friend, and I love you."

"I know. I love you, too. More than you will ever know," he shared.

We've gotten in the habit of having long chats. He loves to meet me here at the beach. It's quiet here and we can talk without any disruptions. We talk about everything from world events, to parenting and everyday challenges. His words are always loving. Sometimes, they are filled with humor, sometimes direct, and sometimes wrapped in parables, allowing me time to figure them out. I never quite know what to expect, but I do know he is everything in my life.

"I've been struggling with something," I said as I prepared my courage to ask a difficult question.

Certainty gently encouraged me. "Go ahead. I have seen the struggle within you for a long time, and you are safe to ask me anything."

"I find myself thinking about my life four years ago. Where were you in my darkest hour? Where were you during those awful years? I couldn't hear your voice back then. I didn't know you, and I was lost. I was alone. Why couldn't you step in and help me? Why did I have to suffer for all those years?"

Certainty patiently listened to my painful questions. I could feel his anguish, which was like that of a parent who desperately loves his struggling child.

"I was always there. Nothing hurt me more than to watch you go through all of that alone. My pain was greater than yours." His voice expressed the tone of an aching heart.

"*But where were you?*" I desperately needed to understand.

"Before you were born, you made an agreement with the Lord to accept a gift. You were not allowed to be born without this gift. What you do with this gift throughout your life is entirely up to you. You can use it to bring blessings or untold pain. *This gift also requires you to invite me into your life.* I am not allowed in until you invite me."

"What is this gift?" I was very confused.

"Free will."

"I still don't understand. Where does free will come into the picture when something terrible *happens* to us? That's what I'm asking—why weren't you around then?" I continued to plead.

"You may not be able to control everything that happens to you, or to those you love, but you can always control your reactions and feelings. That is free will. Free will dictates that I am not allowed into your life until you invite me. Your free will chose to react and feel suffering. *You chose* to almost give up," he explained.

I sat there for a long time, thinking about what he said. Slowly, I began to put the pieces together. "Until the day I prayed to God and He sent me to Saint Patrick's?" I wondered out loud.

"Yes, that was the first time you invited me in. You finally asked for guidance and opened the door. You see you don't even have to throw the door wide-open; even a tiny crack, and I will rush in," he promised me.

"That day, I prayed to God. I went looking for a Bible, but instead I found myself in New York City at the cathedral. How did that happen? Why didn't God teach me through His scripture?" I asked.

"Because you weren't ready. In His infinite wisdom, He knew you were just not ready to understand any scriptural passage. He needed a more creative plan. He sent you to Saint Patrick's because He knew you would feel safe there and would be open to receiving His light."

"I think I understand," I said as I thought about this.

"That is another law of the universe. You can't receive an answer you're simply not ready for. When you pray, sometimes the answer is not what you're expecting. That's because the answer is always designed to give you what you *need,* not what *you think you want*," he added for extra emphasis.

"When I prayed in Jerusalem in front of the icon of the Virgin Mary, she answered my prayer directly and sent me Chris," I thought aloud.

"Do you know why?" he asked.

"What do you mean why? I prayed, and she answered my prayer," I said.

"Listen...*do you know why your prayer was answered directly*—and not in some mysterious way that many people affectionately have come to call 'blessings in disguise.' Have you finally come to truly understand why your prayer was answered directly?" he challenged me.

I didn't want to disappoint him, so I thought very carefully and for a long time. I finally said, "I know forgiveness had a lot to do with it. It was a blockage in my life that controlled me."

"That's very good, but it's only part of the answer," he said.

This was a lot harder than I thought. I didn't know what to say, so I finally spoke from my heart. "When I stood in front of her in Jerusalem, I heard her speak to me. I *heard* her, the same way I can *hear* you. She said, 'Pray to me. Pray with love in your heart, and I promise to wipe away your tears and answer your prayers.' *I heard these words spoken to me*. That's what I did. I prayed, and she kept her promise. She wiped away my tears and answered my prayer."

"Yes." He paused. "When you were told to 'Pray with love in your heart,' *you responded by praying for others first. That is the reason your prayer was answered."*

I suppose I never consciously understood the mystery of that day. *You prayed for others first....* It seems like an easy lesson to learn, but it is much harder to live it every day. I had been so caught up in my own life lately that, too often, I had simply forgotten to pray for others.

He began to laugh. "Remember, I can hear your thoughts. Yes, it is very hard to live this every day.

Just take one step at a time. Think about others a little more every day and about yourself a little less."

I thought about this honestly and admitted to myself that I could improve in that department. I needed to focus more on praying for others. This thought drifted first to those around me, to my community, and then to the world we live in. I had opened my heart to praying for those who were suffering, and at that moment, my next question popped into my head, "Why do so many good people have to suffer?"

"Everyone has free will. When the actions of someone else's free will bring pain and suffering into your life, the purpose is to provide you with the opportunity to use your free will to bring light into the world."

"Is pain necessary to grow spiritually?"

"No. This is a very common misperception. You were not born to suffer and experience pain. *Your destiny is to experience a life of happiness, joy, and the greatest eternal love.*"

"How?" I wondered.

"Are you happy?" he asked me.

"Of course. I'm happier than I've ever been in my life. I'm overwhelmed with happiness, love, and joy."

"Then I'll ask you again: How did you do it?"

He always does this to me, especially when I want an easy answer. He challenges me to think about my own journey and consciously understand the lessons along the way.

"I guess the first step was when I prayed to God and invited him back into my life. Then you came and the miracles in my life began. You have been the answer to everything. You are the reason my life is filled with joy and eternal love. You fill my heart with the desire to share. You are the reason I found my destiny."

He began to laugh like a proud parent whose child has finally accomplished a great task. "Yes."

I was overwhelmed with gratitude.

"My only anguish, the greatest pain in my heart, was not allowing you in my life sooner. I wasted so many years," I confessed.

"I know. Don't dwell on the past with regret, because the past is what brought you here. This has been your journey. Besides, since you always have your free will, you can choose to use this journey to inspire others," he hinted.

I thought deeply about these lessons. There was still so much to learn and understand. "So many people I love just don't have you in their lives. They don't know the secret. They cling to Hope, but they have no idea that you are the answer to everything. How do I help them?" I pleaded for guidance.

"Remember, you cannot interfere with anyone else's free will or force someone to accept me. Hope is wonderful. If your loved ones at least have her, she will do a great job of sustaining them until they are ready to meet me. In the meantime, if they crack open the door, I can always sneak in a few miracles. Like you, your loved ones must use their own free will to accept me unconditionally. They all have their own journeys."

"Thank you," I acknowledged warmly. I was finally beginning to really understand this lesson.

He bowed his head in a humble act of pure love. "I will share with you one more secret," he announced. I was very excited as I prepared myself to hear this wisdom.

"I don't ever need to receive thanks, but you do need to give it," he gently told me.

"I'm not sure I understand the difference."

He paused for a moment and explained, "The difference is simply your consciousness. When you think I need to hear your thanks, you create an opening for Ego to come in and convince you what a wonderful person you are for always giving thanks. When you remind yourself that I don't need to receive your thanks but that you need to give it, you close the door to your Ego."

"I think I understand." I paused to reflect on these words.

"Let me give you a more practical explanation," Certainty began. "Your child is still a baby, but one day you will teach her to say thank you. As a parent, you want her to learn basic manners, but what is more important is that this practice brings the miracle of gratitude into her life. You aren't teaching her because *you want* or *need* the thanks. Do you understand?"

"I do. Let me try again with my new consciousness," I said. I took a deep breath, and with genuine gratitude, I asked, "Will you please accept my thank you?"

"With love," he smiled.

Every time I had a few moments to myself, I reflected on all the lessons my best friend Certainty has been teaching me. Now that I truly understood,

I was ashamed of myself. I was ashamed that I had allowed Doubt to interfere with my journey and convince me that Certainty didn't exist. I was deeply ashamed.

"Can you please forgive me for all those times I denied you? Now I understand that you never abandoned me; it was me—my free will. I was the one who didn't let you in. Please, can you forgive me?"

His voice was filled with deep emotion and love. "You are unconditionally forgiven, *and you are unconditionally loved*."

"Really, it's that easy? After all I've done?"

His look was quite serious; I could feel his love pierce my soul. "Yes, it's that easy. My disciple denied me three times following my arrest, and then shed tears of repentance. Through repentance, you will always be forgiven."

"Your disciple?" My mind was spinning in awe.

"Yes. Who do you think you have been speaking to all this time?"

Yes. Before I was born, She promised to protect me all the days of my life. She has. She has given me the gift of her Son.

Acknowledgements

THE DICTIONARY DEFINES GRATITUDE AS A NOUN, THE STATE of being grateful, thankfulness. In the Bible are many psalms, proverbs, quotes, and parables that only begin to hint at the miracle of gratitude in our lives. I will travel through some of my favorite quotes in the Bible to humbly offer my gratitude and thanks.

Psalm 107:1 - (NIV) *Give thanks to the LORD, for he is good; his love endures forever.* I most humbly offer my thanks to the Lord, our Creator, for all that is and ever was.

Timothy 1:12 (NIV) - *I thank Christ Jesus our Lord, who has given me strength, that he considered me faithful, appointing me to his service.* I most humbly offer my thanks to the Lord Jesus Christ for His love and promise of eternal life.

Revelation 12:1 (NIV) - *A great and wondrous sign appeared in heaven: a woman clothed with the sun, with the moon under her feet and a crown of twelve stars on her head.* I most humbly offer my thanks to the Blessed Virgin Mary for protecting me all the days of my life and delivering me to my destiny.

I humbly thank all the angels and saints in heaven who have lifted my prayers and assisted me in every area of my life.

My spiritual journey has blessed me with many communities and beautiful, highly elevated souls whose spiritual guidance, love, and wisdom have changed mylife forever.

Thank you, thank you, thank you to:

Saint Patrick's Cathedral, for bringing the light back into my life. The Syriac Orthodox Church and most especially Saint Mark's Convent in Jerusalem and His Eminence Archbishop Mor Severious Malke Mourad for the prayers, honor, and love you have extended to my family. The lady (an Angel in disguise) at Saint Mark's Convent who opened those doors to me and told me to pray to our Blessed Mother. Eliyahu and Debbie Jian for your love, guidance, and wisdom. The Rosa Mystica House of Prayer in Edmeston, NY, for the answered prayers and blessings you have brought into our lives. Father Darius Koszyk for bestowing upon us the honor of marriage. Father Gode Iwale for your continued prayers and support. Our parishes the Roman Catholic Church of Saint Dominic's in Oyster Bay,

Saint Joan of Arc in Boca Raton, and Saint Anthony's in Fort Lauderdale.

The Lord sends us many teachers along our journey to share His light and wisdom. I am honored and grateful for each of these communities and individuals.

My journey to live this story included many to whom I am eternally thankful.

Thank you, thank you, thank you to:

Mom and Dad for simply everything. I love you beyond words. Dad, I miss you every day of my life. My soul mate, my husband, and dearest love, Christopher. You are the light in my life, and I am the luckiest and happiest woman in the world. Our three beautiful gifts from heaven, my stepdaughter Abbey, daughters Josephine and Victoria, and our dog Bailey. You are simply my everything and the greatest loves of our lives. My sisters and my brother, who have shared much of this journey. Aunt Marlene, thank you for taking me to Jerusalem and coming back there for us. You will never know how much it means to me. Joseph von Zwehl for all your love and support and for your remarkable legacy, which inspires us to be better people every single day. You are so loved and missed. Noreen von Zwehl for being a most wonderful and supportive mother-in-law. Sean von Zwehl, for being our angel when we needed one. Mark von Zwehl for supporting us.

My journey to write this story and publish this book included a team whose hard work, contributions, and advice have been indispensible.

Thank you, thank you, thank you to:

My publishing team at Johann Press. My editor Sarah Aschenbach for her collaborative editing approach, wonderful advice, and for helping me become a better writer. My graphic designer Karrie Ross for developing the cover design and interior layout. My website developer Cenay Nailor for her technical expertise. My entire publicity team at Smith Publicity. All the readers and literary reviewers who received advance copies for your advice and feedback.

My journey also includes my dearest friends who have simply loved and supported me and who are always in my heart.

Thank you, thank you, thank you to:

My dearest friends in the world. You know who you are. I love you for always being there for me. Todd, for inviting me to the party. All my Twitter followers, Facebook fans, and Facebook friends for your encouragement and support.

My gratitude and thanks extend to all the authors who preceded me, who have traveled their own journeys and discovered great wisdom. Thank you for sharing your gifts with the world. Every single day

I learn from the great minds of the past and present, and I thank you all.

Finally, I thank each of you, my readers. Thank you for picking this book up and sharing this journey with me. I pray you are blessed with answered prayers, miracles, and unconditional love in your life. I pray you live a life filled with Certainty.

I am so blessed, humbled, and honored to have you all in my life. Thank you.

A Special Prayer

In Loving Honor of Pope Francis
The Prayer of Saint Francis

Lord, make me an instrument of your peace,
Where there is hatred, let me sow love;
Where there is injury, pardon;
Where there is doubt, faith;
Where there is despair, hope;
Where there is darkness, light;
Where there is sadness, joy.

O Divine Master,
grant that I may not so much seek to be consoled, as to console;
to be understood, as to understand;
to be loved, as to love.
For it is in giving that we receive.
It is in pardoning that we are pardoned,
and it is in dying that we are born to Eternal Life.

Amen.